100 Ways to Train the Perfect Dog

P9-CFP-278

100 Ways to Train the Perfect Dog

Sarah Fisher &
Marie Miller

David and Charles

Dedicated to Gem (24th February 1994–30th January 2008), Sean's friend, companion and soul mate: a very special Golden Retriever who truly was the perfect dog.

A DAVID & CHARLES BOOK
Copyright © David & Charles Limited 2008
David & Charles is an F+W Media Inc. company
4700 East Galbraith Road
Cincinnati, OH 45236

First published in the UK in 2008
Reprinted 2009

Text copyright © Sarah Fisher and Marie Miller 2008
Cover photograph © Beth Mallon 2008
www.bethmallonphotography.com
All other photographs © David & Charles Limited 2008

Sarah Fisher and Marie Miller have asserted their right to
be identified as authors of this work in accordance with the
Copyright, Designs and Patents Act, 1988.

All rights reserved. No part of this publication may be
reproduced, stored in a retrieval system, or transmitted,
in any form or by any means, electronic or mechanical,
by photocopying, recording or otherwise, without prior
permission in writing from the publisher.

Dog handling is not without risk, and while the author and
publishers have made every attempt to offer accurate and
reliable information to the best of their knowledge and belief,
it is presented without any guarantee. The author and
publishers therefore disclaim any liability incurred in connection
with using the information contained in this book.

A catalogue record for this book is available from the
British Library.

ISBN-10: 978-0-7153-2941-2 paperback
ISBN-13: 0-7153-2941-3 paperback

Printed in China by SNP Leefung
for David & Charles
Brunel House   Newton Abbot   Devon

Commissioning Editor: Jane Trollope
Desk Editor: Emily Rae
Project Editor: Jo Weeks
Art Editor: Martin Smith
Production Controller: Kelly Smith
Photographer: Bob Atkins

Visit our website at www.davidandcharles.co.uk

David & Charles books are available from all good bookshops;
alternatively you can contact our Orderline on 0870 9908222
or write to us at FREEPOST EX2 110, D&C Direct, Newton
Abbot, TQ12 4ZZ (no stamp required UK only); US customers
call 800-289-0963 and Canadian customers call 800-840-5220.

Contents

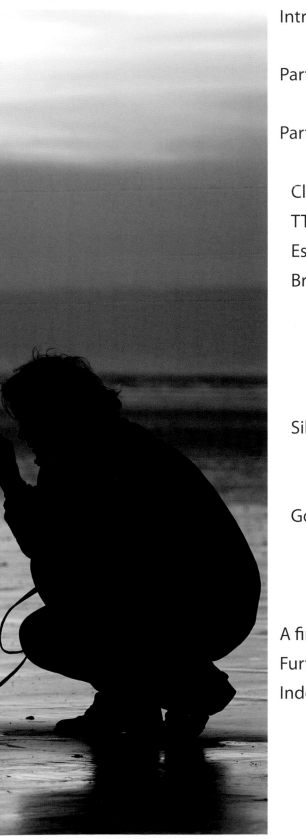

Why perfect?

In truth, dogs are already perfect as they all have many natural abilities such as herding, retrieving, protecting livestock and so on. They are social animals that can mix successfully with a variety of other species including humans, cats, horses, livestock and smaller creatures, and live happily in a range of environments. However, like children, dogs need to learn how to behave appropriately. As owners it is wholly our responsibility to help our dogs develop good social skills to ensure they are well mannered, confident and content.

Your dog doesn't want to become a president, but he would really like to work. His working skills are determined by his breed type and have been fine-tuned over countless years of selective breeding. He is a master at survival and is a thinking, sentient being.

Dogs enjoy learning and continue to learn throughout their life. Well-trained dogs are a pleasure to own. They are true partners and a much-loved, integral part of family life. They are obedient, joyful, entertaining, clever, content and fun, and they enrich the lives of their human companions on many levels.

Training does not mean you create an automaton that does not dare to put a paw out of place. Training is simply teaching your dog good manners to keep you sane and him safe while also giving him appropriate mental and physical stimulation to ensure he leads a happy and healthy life. Every dog has the ability to come when he is called, to lie down and settle when appropriate, to sit and stay, to walk calmly on the leash, to leave personal items alone and to greet people and other animals in a suitable fashion.

How you help your dog adapt to life in the human world is up to you. You may decide to try agility, working trials or doggy dancing; or you may prefer simply to work with him at home. Regardless of your aims, you will need to be a fair and effective teacher to help him fulfill his true potential, whether he will become a title winner of the future or be the

If you do not have the time to train a dog but still want a faithful hound – purchase one of these

Dogs can be content in a variety of situations – Little Finch lives happily on a canal boat and greets everyone who walks along the towpath

Dogs love being successful. Teaching them to work over obstacles, find hidden toys and treats and so on will enhance their physical, emotional and mental wellbeing

champion of your heart. The only golden rules that apply to dog training are to be calm, creative, consistent, patient and kind.

You will be amazed at what your dog can learn and perhaps more importantly, what you can teach him yourself. Dog training is not the preserve of a few highly skilled individuals who were virtually born in a whelping box. Anyone can do it and this includes you. Working with your dog using the techniques described in this book will also deepen the rapport between you, and open up wonderful interspecies communication. Your dog will become more co-ordinated and self-controlled, and will want to be with you, work with you, and listen to your every word (well, most of the time anyhow). Yes! It is possible for you to become more interesting than that squirrel in the park and more exciting than the mailman. You will also find that you learn skills that will enhance every area of your life.

TIME IS ON YOUR SIDE

The earlier you can teach your dog the better, because there will be less that he needs to un-learn. But older dogs can still learn new skills and even well-established unwanted behaviours can be dramatically reduced with time, knowledge and patience. While older dogs may be slower to learn due to changes in their physical health, the old adage that you cannot teach an old dog new tricks is simply not true.

Halo is 11 years old and still enjoys learning new skills

Orsa and Naomi – training dogs is not rocket science. It is great fun, extremely rewarding and should not be hard work for you or your dog

Part One
Why train your dog?

A well-trained dog is a flexible dog that can process new information and adjust to a variety of situations. We owe it to our dogs to ensure that they are happy, appropriately stimulated, well-fed and looked after while in our care; we also need to teach them how to be socially acceptable and to be able to adapt with minimum stress should their home life alter.

The benefits to humans of owning a dog are well documented, but owning an untrained, bored, insecure dog is unlikely to reduce your risk of stress-related diseases: many a well-intentioned, animal-lover has been reduced to a wreck by the antics of the boisterous four-legged canine monster they invited into their home. An out-of-control dog can also be costly. He may destroy your house, shred the interior of your car or cause injury to another person or animal simply by being unruly. Other anti-social behaviour, such as excessive barking when left alone, can also cause problems, and as all behaviours are linked, time spent educating your dog will help keep him calm and relaxed, whether you are with him or not.

Dogs love going out and about – Cookie is enjoying a walk on the beach with Sarah

What is a trainer?

It is important you realize that a trainer is not just someone who works with dogs on a professional basis. Anyone who lives with an animal is a trainer of sorts, as training does not only occur when you pick up a treat bag, a whistle, a clicker or a leash. Dogs learn by watching us and take their cues from our body language and behaviour and our own responses to stimuli. We are training our dogs every minute we are with them, whether we are aware of it or not. So, as we are constantly educating our dogs anyhow, it makes sense to shape this natural learning process into something that is productive, fun and rewarding, regardless of our long-term goals.

However, it can be helpful to take your dog to some training classes, particularly if you are a first-time dog owner: you will both learn a lot, which will come in useful when you want to continue training on your own. Take care how you choose your trainer. Some people train dogs using negative reinforcement: this is an aversive technique that is used to punish the dog until an unacceptable behaviour ceases. Others train by using positive reinforcement and by marking and rewarding the behaviours that they want, which is not only kinder but also far more effective (see box opposite and also way 37, p.81).

TRAINING TERMS

So. What do all the training terms mean to you and your dog? Well it depends on what your dog has already learned. Ideally 'heel work' means that your dog works closely by your side, either on or off the leash, but for some dogs 'heel work' means that they attach themselves resolutely to the bottom of a trouser leg with their teeth. 'Send away' for some people means teaching their dog to go to a mark on cue, but for others it may mean that visitors are sent running hysterically back to the sanctuary of their car with an errant hound in hot pursuit. And then, of course, there's 'down' – it should not be the way you feel when you think about your relationship with your dog.

(Right) Bud is a gorgeous Doberman whose owners had to make the difficult but correct decision to rehome him. He has slotted in easily with Sarah's family because he was so beautifully trained using positive techniques. Bud still sees his original family and is a very happy hound

Dogs learn by watching everything around them

A brief outline of learning theory

There is plenty of misunderstanding about training terms and meanings, so here they are in a nutshell.

POSITIVE REINFORCEMENT (R+)

A reward is **added** to increase the likelihood that behaviour will be repeated. An example is rewarding a dog with food if he comes when called. After a few repetitions the dog will learn to return quickly to his owner in anticipation of the reward – what a wonderful way for a dog to learn.

NEGATIVE REINFORCEMENT (R-)

An aversive is **removed** to increase the likelihood that behaviour will be repeated. An example of this is to apply force to push a dog into a sit, removing the physical pressure only when he sits. The dog learns to sit to avoid the physical pressure – not the most pleasant way to learn.

POSITIVE PUNISHMENT (P+)

An aversive is **added** to stop behaviour. An example of this is to use a spray collar to stop a dog from barking. The collar is activated by the sound and ceases working when the dog stops barking. However, the distress of the punishment is likely to linger and the dog may become fearful, anticipating something unpleasant (the spray) whenever he hears a similar hissing sound from any source. This is not a pleasant way to train a dog.

NEGATIVE PUNISHMENT (P-)

A potential reward is **removed** to stop behaviour. An example of this is to turn or move away without looking at or speaking to a dog that is barking for attention. He will learn that his undesirable behaviour lost the potential reward (the attention of the person). This is the only form of punishment that has a place in modern dog training.

CLASSICAL CONDITIONING

Using this method an involuntary response from a dog can be paired with an unrelated and neutral stimulus. It was made famous by Pavlov who noticed that dogs salivate before feeding, a response not under the dog's control (unconditioned response). He then began to pair the neutral sound of a bell with feeding and the dogs began salivating at the sound in anticipation of food. A bell had now become the conditioned stimulus. The sound of the clicker is often introduced using Classical Conditioning in preparation for using it as a valuable Operant Conditioning tool.

OPERANT CONDITIONING

A dog learns that his own actions influence the consequences of his behaviour. People often ask why their dog repeats a behaviour that they feel they have punished before, so it helps to understand if you see Operant Conditioning through the dog's eyes.

For example, when a dog jumps up for a fuss and successfully gains attention, even if he is punished by the person shouting at him or pushing him away, the reward (i.e. attention) outweighs the consequence and it is therefore an effective behaviour, which will be repeated by the dog. On the other hand if the dog is consistently ignored when he jumps up and only rewarded with attention for keeping four feet on the floor, he will learn that jumping up is not an effective method of getting somebody to notice him. The consequence of his actions will influence him not to jump up to get attention.

A short story

If you find it difficult to understand the difference between positive and negative reinforcement, imagine this: you have joined a company where no-one speaks your language and no-one has told you what to do. You have not been given any training and your job description is vague. You cannot call a friend to ask for help so you try to work things out by yourself.

You entertain yourself because no one has told you what to do

You run around offering to do a bit of everything because you have so many natural, wonderful skills and so much energy. Everyone seems to disapprove. When you leap about frantically trying to protect the property, greet clients by planting a huge smacker on each cheek, barge in on the board meetings, grab everything that your colleagues leave lying around, and help yourself to what you think is your share of the corporate lunch, the company director either hits you or drags you from your desk and shuts you in another room. You shout at him, but he has no idea what you are trying to say. He leaves you alone. You have no direction, no defined tasks and you are confused. You are also getting bored. You start doodling on the in-house publications and making pretty shapes from the paper in the bin. Your boss does not give you anything to do but it also seems he does not want you working out a way to fill those endless hours.

In time, you learn that it is pointless trying to communicate with other members of the team and your boss seems happier because you are quiet. You have not submitted.

Dogs like to know their role

Your new boss tells you oh so very clearly that you are his PA!

You have given up. Suddenly, your boss starts to talk to you again and you are soooooo excited that he is engaging with you once more that you cannot override a burning desire to hug him. And you find yourself back in that boring, uninspiring, lonely place once more. You discover the art of learned helplessness, and depression becomes your middle name.

If you are lucky, your boss will fire you, or better still, go on a cracking course that teaches him alternative and more productive ways of working with the people he employs. Suddenly the Big Cheese understands you. He can communicate! Yipppeeee! He lets you know very calmly and very clearly that you are his PA. Hurrah! He teaches you how to accomplish every task that he expects you to do and he does this, one simple step at a time. He smiles at you. He is proud of you. He thanks you. He gives you presents – a super duper stapler and a shiny pen. He takes you places. Every time you do your job correctly you are praised. If you make a mistake your boss does not shout at you or ignore you for the rest of the week, because he knows it must have been his fault; he obviously didn't teach you well enough or he confused you.

You learn something new every day so you are never bored. Your boss gives you lunch breaks and he never overworks you. You love your job. You love your boss. And best of all it seems as though he loves you too. If you do occasionally slip back into your old habits, you are reminded gently that you do not to have to run the security section nor be the first to do the meet-and-greets, and are redirected to your beautiful desk so that you can perform the job you have been employed to do. Everyone is happy and everything

one huge success. You are finally appreciated for the unique and loyal being that you are and all is well.

Many dogs are living through the first part of this scenario because their owners simply do not know what else to do. Ignoring a dog and restricting exercise, or punishing him for unwanted behaviour will not help him learn. Think about how your dog might view his life with you and look at yourself through his eyes. Would you understand what was being asked of you? Would you enjoy the partnership? Would you want to lead the lifestyle that you have chosen for him? Looking at ourselves in this way helps us be fairer in our expectations and more aware of our dog's needs.

Always remember your dog did not choose to live with you: you picked him.

If you were your dog would you enjoy the life you have picked for him?

13

Why things go wrong

Sadly, not every human–dog relationship has a happy ending. The majority of dogs that get into trouble live with first-time owners who have been unable (or unwilling) to spend the necessary time building a solid relationship with their dog. Sometimes it may be a case of the owner inadvertently training inappropriate behaviour through rough games that arouse or frighten the dog.

Dogs also run into problems because their owners do not understand their needs and misinterpret and/or mislabel their behaviours and responses. A dog 'misbehaves' (in the eyes of the human) primarily because he is bored and because there is a lack of clear guidance and direction. He has many instinctive desires and natural drives and if he has no outlet for these he will be frustrated; a stressed dog is a problem dog. The majority of dogs that find their way into dog shelters lack basic obedience skills, and have become confused and defensive as a result.

In the extreme, dogs can become dangerous. They can bite and they can kill, and attacks on people and other animals

Many dogs end up in the shelter (left) because they are untrained (top). Training (above) will increase a shelter dog's chances of finding a new home

are not limited to specific breeds. Different breeds do have specific traits that have been encouraged through years of selective breeding but, in truth, no single breed is more aggressive than another. A high proportion of dog bites happen in the home: if your dog is showing any signs of reactive behaviour towards family members, other people or other animals get professional help immediately.

If your dog consistently behaves in a way that you don't like, look thoroughly at every aspect of his life. Something is amiss. He may need a thorough health check or you may need to change something in the way you manage him. Be honest with yourself and trust your instincts. You know your dog and if you do run into problems, get help from someone who uses kind and positive training techniques and who will work with you on a one-to-one basis. Sending your dog away for corrective training is not the answer.

Raised hair around the base of the tail can be linked to tension in the back

Holly carries tension through her whole body, which makes it hard for her to relax and walk in balance on the leash (above). Changing the slip leash for a double clipped leash and using TTouches on her body and around her head helps her to settle very quickly (below)

The posture-behaviour connection

Postural habits are set down from a very early age, and the link between posture and behaviour should not be overlooked. A dog that carries tension through his hindquarters, for example, is more likely to be timid and noise-sensitive than a dog that is relaxed through the lower back, hips and tail. Tension in this area can also trigger the flight/fight reflex.

Puppies may have problems stemming from a difficult birth. Accidents, forceful handling, dragging a dog by his collar, persistent pulling on a leash, excessive rough-and-tumble play and so on can also set up problem areas in the body that will affect the way the dog thinks, feels and learns.

Use the handling exercises (ways 10, 11, 12, 50 and 51) to check for sensitive or 'no-go' areas and the Tellington TTouches (pp.35–38) to help release tension and reduce any concerns that your dog may have about contact.

Dogs with tension through the back may find it hard to settle and will be sensitive to contact in this area

What every dog owner needs to know

Whether you are new to dogs or you have a always had a dog around the place, there are a few things that you need to understand about your basic canine.

(Above and below) Dogs use a complex system of body language with each other and with other species, including humans

How to approach a dog

In our human social world, it is considered polite to approach another person from the front, to look at them and maintain eye contact when we interact. But for many dogs, this type of approach can be intimidating, particularly if the dog has no chance to 'escape'. Be aware that staring directly at a dog, leaning over him or hugging him may trigger defensive or fearful responses. Until you have developed a bond and he trusts you not to hurt him, it is safer to approach your dog from the side and to use the back of your hand to initiate contact. Keep your eyes 'soft' by lowering your eyelids a little. If he is still worried, glance at him, then look away, with your chin lowered and with a slightly bowed head. If you find that you have locked eyes with a dog, blinking slowly a couple of times often helps to let him know that you are not intending to threaten him.

How dogs learn

Dogs are born with a natural desire to learn new skills. They work on a motive-and-reward basis, as do humans. Dogs are also able to piece together sequences, which makes them really quite easy to train if we, as their guardians, get things right.

Dogs naturally repeat behaviours that gain a reward and should therefore give up offering behaviours that earned them nothing. Easy? Well not necessarily because, as well as all the other exciting or yummy things you give him, your dog sees getting your attention as a reward.

For example, if you take advantage of his quiet moments to catch up on phonecalls or jobs around the home without acknowledging that your dog is behaving in the way you like, he may learn to seek your attention by snatching your diary, incessantly barking or digging in your favourite flower bed. As far as a dog is concerned, negative attention is better than no attention at all. So…don't ignore him when he is lying quietly in his bed or crate or playing on his own in the garden. Praise him when he is offering these desirable behaviours and give him a treat, even if you have not actually asked him to do anything specific, and he will know he is doing the right thing.

How dogs communicate

Dogs use their body posture to communicate with other dogs and humans. In order to be good teachers we need to be excellent students, and learning your dog's body language will help you to understand him on a new level. All owners recognize the more apparent dog language, such as growling, whining, or barking, and you may be familiar with the variety of barks your dog uses to express himself, but dogs also use very subtle body language. (Some of these have been noted by Turid Rugaas, and her book *On Talking Terms with Dogs* is a recommended read for anyone who owns or works with dogs.)

Always look at a dog's responses in the context in which they are happening. For example, lip licking can be a sign of anticipation if the dog is waiting for his food or expecting a treat and this is usually accompanied by bright, shiny eyes and forward-pointing ears. However, a dog that drops his head and flattens his ears while licking his lips is probably feeling threatened or unsure. Sniffing the ground and scratching can be a sign that a dog is taking time out because he is unsure, is tired or is getting confused. If your dog constantly scratches his neck when you are trying to teach him new skills, you may be overloading him. Do some TTouches (pp.35–38), go back to an earlier exercise or give him a complete break.

Take the time to observe your dog when he is in a new environment, also watch him when you approach him, work with him and when he greets other dogs and people. If you look for early signs of concern, you can take the appropriate action to ensure that he remains as calm and as confident as possible. Dog-watching can become a fascinating pastime, too.

A bright expression and forward ears reveal that this lip licking is a sign of anticipation

Does your dog see you as part of his pack?

Do you know any dogs that put leashes on other dogs? Take another dog to the groomers? Drive another dog to the park so that they career around together with the wind whizzing past their ears? If your answer is 'no', well done, you have successfully dispelled a common myth. Dogs know the difference between humans and other dogs; they do not think we are dogs. If your answer is 'yes', please send us his address so that we can ask him to help us write the next book!

While social structure is important, there is a lot of misleading information bandied about regarding pack, rank and hierarchy, which can cause problems for both the dog and his family. Dogs look for, and respond to, guidance. If left to their own devices, they will naturally make up their own entertainment and start taking things into their own paws.

As with any partnership or group situation, someone has to be the leader. You do not have to become a dictator and rule the canine household with a rod of iron, but you do need to be calmly in control and to teach your dog how to behave appropriately.

There may be times when you have to let him know that his behaviour is unacceptable, but to be an effective leader you need to show him how you do want him to behave and praise him for doing as you ask, rather than punishing him when he does something that you do not want him to do. (See also Setting boundaries, p.24, and When you need to correct your dog, p.32.)

A NATURAL LEADER

If you spend time bonding with your dog and training him using the techniques in this book you will naturally become an important leader and motivator in his life. You will not need to eat before he does (think how huge every trainer would be if they had to eat a biscuit before giving a dog a treat), withhold contact, or win every game, in order to maintain your social status. He will happily and readily do as you ask.

Work through the techniques in this book and you will naturally become important in your dog's life

A deep lasting relationship is something that is earned: it is not an automatic right

Labelling dogs

A label placed on a dog can be very difficult to remove, and many dogs that are labelled 'aggressive' are exhibiting responses more appropriately described as 'defensive'. We think that everyone who owns or works with dogs should be encouraged to keep a dictionary on hand to ensure that they use the correct word when describing dog behaviour, as many terms and words are used inaccurately! It is not that we want to excuse anti-social behaviour, far from it; but if we misinterpret a dog's responses we limit our ability to truly understand and help him.

Many dogs labelled as 'dominant' are insecure and unsure of their boundaries. A true 'leader' dog does not need to engage in unnecessary fights, resolutely hoard all resources or continuously prowl the fence line on the look out for intruders. Why? Because he has confidence and self-control, and knows that should he need, or want, to take appropriate action, he can. He will be able to convey his feelings with a look or a change in body posture rather than a full on assault and he will also be able to differentiate between an actual or potential threat and respond accordingly.

Orsa is a Maremma – she is a guardian dog but is extremely sociable with people and other animals

Getting the basics right

Whether you are just about to bring a dog into your home, or you have decided to start anew on your relationship, it is important to be sure that his surroundings are appropriate and that you have all the equipment you need.

Environment

Make sure the environment is safe. Trailing electrical wires, mobile and portable phones, clutter, shoes, clothing, childrens' toys and so on can be very inviting to a young or bored dog, sometimes with disastrous consequences. Some garden plants are poisonous and, of course, chocolate and various common household and garden products, such as slug pellets, anti-freeze and pesticides, can be fatal. There is plenty of information on the Internet regarding toxic plants and household products so carry out research to ensure your home and garden are dog-friendly. Crate training (way 1) will help you to keep your dog in a safe chew-free environment when you are out and at night.

Cookie is really happy to spend tine in her indoor kennel and even chooses to enter it on her own when she wants to rest

19

Equipment

To work effectively with your dog when using this book you will need: a clicker, a whistle, a target stick, a mat, treats and a long line (see photograph). You will need a grooming kit, which might include a sheepskin mitt and a Jelly Scrubber™, made by Tail Tamers (see p.141).

First and foremost you need a flat collar, a harness and a double-clipped leash as these enable you to have more control with dogs that pull, lunge, walk on their hind legs or leap about when on the leash and diminish the chances of accidentally jarring your dog's neck or hurting him in any way.

Toys and appropriate play

Dogs build close bonds and relationships through play and physical contact. In the litter, puppies learn to play games to establish how to possess articles, and how to give them up, including the best teat and a comfy spot to sleep. It is important to play with your dog and equally important to set boundaries for play.

Try to establish two types of toy for your dog – ones that are safe for them to play with alone, and others that you can play with too. For the first type, rubber Kong™ toys (see p.141) or similar are ideal because they can be stuffed with treats that will occupy him safely and give him an

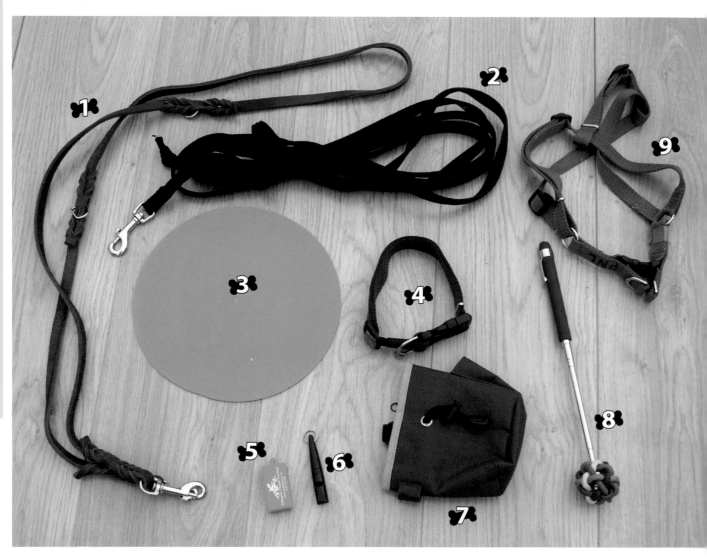

You will need some specific equipment to work through the exercises in this book: **1** double-clipped leash, **2** long line, **3** mat, **4** flat collar, **5** clicker, **6** whistle, **7** treat pouch, **8** target stick, **9** harness

Marie and Maisie demonstrating a collar, harness and double-clipped leash. This combination provides plenty of choices when it comes to teaching your dog how to move in balance on the leash

Cookie is having great fun playing with a squeaky toy

Stuffed with treats, rubber Kongs™ enable a dog to amuse himself

important outlet for chewing (please read the important safety note, right). Let your dog know that you are pleased to see him play with or chew these toys, but avoid playing a shared game with him as ideally you want him to learn how to entertain himself safely. Your dog will probably try to encourage you to play by bringing a chew toy and dropping it on your feet or in your lap. Just be neutral; do not make an issue of it or acknowledge his action. Get up casually and put on the kettle or look out of the window. The toy will drop to the floor and the dog will soon accept that his chew toy is not an effective tool for gaining your attention.

In addition to the chew toys, you will need a few mutual play toys, such as a ball on a rope, a tuggy toy, a squeaky toy and so on. You can also buy some games from the range of interactive dog toys developed by Nina Ottosson (see also p.141).

Put these toys out of the dog's reach and when you want to play with him, get them out and invite him to play a shared game (see 'Playing a shared game', way 18). If he chooses not to, just pretend you are having tremendous fun with the toy, then put it away and carry on with what you were doing before (or go and reassure any spectators that you have not lost your marbles). If he does join in, start teaching the

TOYS – A VERY IMPORTANT SAFETY NOTE

When purchasing a toy that can be stuffed with treats make sure you pick one that has a hole all the way through it. When a dog plays with a toy that has a hole at each end and is solid in the middle, his mouth can create a vacuum that may trap his tongue inside the toy, causing it to swell. This will result in panic and distress; it could cause serious injury to your dog and may even be fatal.

shared game and end it while he still wants to play, so that you always leave him wanting more. This will help maintain his interest in the toys, and in his interaction with you.

21

Most dogs love a bit of variety in their exercise routine

Exercise

Walking your dog is not just about giving him exercise; it also provides mental stimulation. He gets to check out new scents, become an authority on the local wildlife and to see what is going on his neighbourhood. A visit to the park, the beach or the country will keep him more mentally satisfied than an hour's blast around the property he already knows. If a dog is reluctant to venture outside during excessive heat or in three feet of snow, however,

the exercises listed in this book will help to keep him active on all levels. If you are the one that is reluctant to brave the elements, remember there is no such thing as bad weather, just unsuitable clothing!

Games to avoid

Avoid play fighting, especially with large breeds and where children, elderly or disabled people come into regular contact with your dog. This is a game of strength and generally involves mouthing and play biting (from the dog). It is not fair to engage in games that may get your dog into trouble if he tries to play them with somebody else or that might encourage behaviour you cannot cope with.

Chasing is often encouraged when children are playing and the dog attempts to join the game. It also occurs when there is unsupervised, rough play with other dogs and animals. It is important that your dog does not learn to view children and other animals as moving chew toys. Leave a light webbing leash trailing so that you can quietly pick it up and call a 'time out' during play sessions. If children are playing fast, noisy games it is unfair to expect your dog to remain calm.

Chasing games can cause problems when the dog picks up something he should not have. Dogs learn very quickly that they are able to keep possession of a 'trophy' by moving faster and squeezing into smaller places than a human can. They also learn to steal items that get your immediate attention. Try to ensure that your dog has more fun if he comes when he is called than he does if he runs away (if you are already experiencing this type of problem, see ways 18, 19 and 20).

Exercise provides necessary mental and physical stimulation

If your puppy gets overexcited and begins to rip up a soft toy or tear a squeaky toy to get the squeak out, end the game straightaway. This is a 'killing' game that can become over-the-top and is potentially aggressive.

Socialization

Socialization is important. Even if you live a solitary life you still need to ensure that your dog responds to basic commands, sees plenty of sights and has the opportunity to meet other animals and people so that a trip to the vet or a stay in a boarding kennel does not blow his mind or cause upset to other beings. It is also worth teaching your dog to spend time alone, even if there is always someone around, as circumstances do change and it is always possible that an overnight stay at the vet may be required at some point. It is also important that your dog has time to play with other dogs.

As hard as we try to understand our dogs and shape their behaviour so that they live happily alongside their human companions, nothing takes the place of a romp with another canine friend. Join a club, or meet up with local dogs for a hike or a game in the park. You can even arrange play dates for your hound. (Ways 37–48 all focus on socializing your dog.)

Cookie thinks hands are toys, and her teeth cause serious bruises. She needs to be re-educated in a way that is fun and rewarding for her (and us)

Dogs enjoy the company of other dogs

Training the family

Communication is the key to any successful relationship and this includes communication between everyone that will be looking after or interacting with the dog and, of course, with the dog himself.

In order to work effectively with your dog, you need to train everyone in the family to ensure that he is not receiving mixed messages. It is unrealistic to expect the dog to learn how he should behave if everyone has a different idea of what constitutes acceptable behaviour. If you want him to settle at night on his own in the kitchen, for example, it will be confusing if someone decides to take him to bed with them because they are feeling in need of a cuddle.

Setting boundaries

Prevention is better than cure and it is only fair to your dog if you establish some ground rules as soon as you bring him home. Once you have consistent boundaries you can afford to be more flexible, but at the beginning of your relationship it is easier to create a structure and routine that your dog understands as it will help him to feel safe and secure.

Everyone in the family needs to be in agreement when it comes to training your dog. Naomi is teaching Cookie appropriate food bowl behaviour to avoid problems developing later on

Planning for the future is vital for a successful and harmonious existence. If you own a young dog, remember he will grow. An enthusiastic puppy that jumps up with great gusto to greet visitors may be endearing in the short term, but if Great Auntie Ethel is felled the moment she walks through the door by a mature, slobbering heavy weight, relationships may become a little strained. The puppy that was once the apple of your eye and a part of every social scene may then be relegated to the yard or back room as he starts to mature, which will frustrate him and give rise to a whole host of other problems.

If you have taken on a rescue dog remember his life is good now because he lives with you. Not every dog that is in the shelter has had a bad experience. Remaining attached to the past is not helpful to a dog, and pity can severely limit our abilities to help him. Even if you know for a fact that he has been badly treated and has developed problems as a result, he is still a dog who would like to learn new skills and who can probably be successfully rehabilitated using the exercises in this book.

Containing and restraining

At some point your dog will probably need to be restrained. It may be necessary for him to be held for a veterinary examination or he may have to be stopped in his tracks if he is shooting through an open door or gate leading on to a busy road. If trust in being handled has been built up over time, he probably won't resist.

When taught in the right way (see way 11, Practise calm containment), your dog will ultimately accept restraint without panicking, but it is not a good way to start your relationship with a puppy, and can trigger fear and confusion. There is a big difference between restraining and containing. Restraining makes a dog stay in place, containing asks the dog to stay. Restraining causes the pup to resist and struggle, and the natural reaction of the nervous system makes the person increase their grip, which will panic the puppy. He will then use everything at his disposal to get free. This is pure survival instinct, but even a tiny puppy can be scary when he is fearful of being restrained. TTouch (see pp.35–38) has wonderful tools to help build the trust required. The techniques used contain, rather than restrain the dog and this method can be used for most situations at the vets as well. Containing encourages patience, calmness and confidence in the handler. The non-habitual movements of TTouch help to quieten the nervous system and improve focus.

Special cases

The exercises in section two (pp.40–139) are designed to help you train all sorts of dogs at all sorts of ages and stages. But there are a few cases where a slightly different approach is needed, or you might need to make allowances.

Puppies

Having a new puppy in your life is an exciting experience, and with careful planning and diligent ownership, your puppy should mature into a wonderful companion who will grace your life for many years. Always remember that you are constantly teaching your puppy through your responses and actions. The simple training tips and techniques in the Bronze and Silver sections of the exercises (see p.39) will ensure that your puppy grows into a well-mannered, obedient, sociable adult.

The early weeks are important in teaching your puppy how to respond to stimulus, and the environment in which your puppy was raised will have some influence on how he

behaves when he first goes out into the big wide world. If he was born in a kennel, he may not have heard everyday household noises before. You do not need to creep about but take into account that the sights, sounds and smells in your home may be a new experience for him.

Clicker training (pp.33–34) and TTouch (pp.35–38) are excellent ways to help your puppy learn and to adapt to new situations and can be invaluable for helping puppies that may not have had the best of starts in life.

Puppies naturally explore what to them is an exciting new world by scent and taste

Puppy rearing can be challenging and sometimes owners feel as if they are always having to chase round after their puppy saying, 'NO!'. Veterinarian and behaviourist Dr Ian Dunbar made a lot of sense when he said, 'There are many "wrong" things that your puppy can do and not that many right things, so why keep it a secret? Teach him how you want him to behave and reward him for doing it!'

If your puppy is doing something you deem to be unacceptable, remember that he is behaving naturally and does not understand that he should not act in this way. Puppies often run into problems because the owner has inadvertently (or deliberately) triggered unwanted responses through lack of understanding and poor education. For example, a puppy that has learnt that human hands and feet are fantastic toys to grab and bite is unlikely to stop this behaviour automatically. Use the containment exercise (way 11), greeting exercises (ways 6 and 15) and play exercises (many) to prevent these problems from developing or escalating.

Puppies are curious and will pick up everything with their mouths

NEVER MAKE ASSUMPTIONS

Many dogs seem to think that they are called 'Oi!'. Others appear totally deaf when their owner says, 'Come' but come running when they hear 'What's this' or 'Sweeties'. (Sarah and Archie think back to their early days together, cough and look sheepish at this point) and sadly it is the dog that is often blamed or punished when his behaviour is inappropriate. While a dose of good old common sense will serve you well it is also important to recognize that common sense isn't always common knowledge.

More than one dog

There is a saying: if you have one dog you own a whole dog, if you have two dogs, you own half a dog and if you have three dogs, you do not own any dog. This may be true for people who have not developed a bond or trained their dogs but multi-dog households do not have to present a problem. Two dogs will provide double the entertainment, and if trained will NOT cause double the trouble.

As Chief Executive of the group, it is your responsibility to help your dogs establish the right relationship:

- Introduce them on neutral territory so that they enter the house together.

- Purchase baby gates for your kitchen and/or a dog crate in case your over-enthusiastic newbie bugs the collar off your existing Right-hand Hound. This gives you a dog-safe chill-out zone where he can go to give your older friend a break.

- Start teaching the newcomer the family boundaries from day one and remember to put aside some time to have quality one-to-one sessions with your first dog too so that he does not feel left out.

- Don't give your first dog the responsibility of educating or minding the newcomer. This is especially important if your first dog lacks boundaries and is untrained.

Multi-dog households do not have to present a problem if the dogs are trained appropriately. All of Sarah's dogs had previous homes and are all good friends. Orsa is a Maremma, Bud is a Doberman who was stressed and lost his hair, which is now growing back, Archie is a lurcher from Battersea and Ginny is an elderly lady, also from Battersea, who was suffering from terrible neglect. She is now fit and well but will never regain a full coat

Cookie and Chilli meet on neutral territory – Marie and Clare walk next to each other at first

They change position so that the dogs are now walking side by side but at a polite and reasonable distance

Clare and Marie keep the leashes loose so that the dogs can greet each other calmly and without being aroused by a tight pull on their collars. Cookie and Chilli are introducing themselves in a very appropriate way

• Make sure your new dog forms his strongest bond with you. Limit unsupervised access to the other dog(s) and wild play during the early days; it is down to you to teach the new member of the team how to behave in an appropriate way. You want him to look to you for direction and see you as the Big Cheese instead of an irrelevant crumbly scrap of Parmesan.

• Hark back to your school days and remember what the teachers told you about copying another pupils' work. Copying does not help you learn anything for yourself – if your dog is only following your other hound when you call them back, he will be totally lost (probably literally so) if your other dog is not around.

• If the existing family dog is unable to control interactions with the newcomer, step in and remove the new dog for a couple of minutes if he behaves inappropriately. This is not to punish the newer dog in any way; it is to diffuse the situation and to prevent your existing dog from learning undesirable behaviours in order to protect himself. If you are consistent in this, your new dog will learn the important art of self-control and will behave appropriately with other dogs and family members.

After their sensible introduction, Cookie and Chilli are having a great time playing together

Dogs also need to learn to walk quietly together and to respect each other's space

Deaf or blind dogs

The majority of dogs start to lose their sight and/or hearing as they age but some may have impaired vision or hearing from birth. Vets used to recommend putting deaf puppies to sleep but fortunately this is not such a common practice these days. Good body awareness is paramount for dogs that are either deaf or blind, so TTouch (pp.35–38) can be hugely beneficial.

Bear in mind that a puppy that was born deaf has no knowledge of anything different. See him as a dog first, and understand his breed type second; the fact that he is deaf should be the last thing to focus on. You will, of course, have to modify some of the training cues, such as recall with a whistle and use of the clicker, but teaching him to watch you by using a cue such as pointing at your eye will help him learn that you want him to focus on you. Hand signals are described in many of the exercises and you can use these to teach him to sit, stand, lie down and so on, and you can mark the desired behaviours with a thumbs-up signal in place of the clicker. You could use a small coloured flag to get his attention and to teach him visual cues (way 9). You can also teach him to recall to a flashlight, which will help you to retrieve him from the garden at night. If he is sleeping, avoid touching him. Hold or place a piece of food by his nose to arouse him from his slumbers without startling him.

Some dogs are born with congenital eye problems that may go undetected. They can be the cause of some house-training problems as the dog may be reluctant to go into the garden at night. They can also cause pain, which will reduce your dog's levels of tolerance. If this is ringing any bells with you, take your dog to the vet for an eye examination. He may need to be referred to a specialist.

If your dog is going blind you can use a bodywrap to help him with spatial awareness (way 10). Talk to him and teach him verbal cues with the clicker to turn left, right and so on. Of course, he still has a nose so the Nina Ottosson interactive dog toys (ways 32, 33, 75 and 76) will be great for maintaining his interest.

Colin was born deaf and ended up in rescue. He is incredibly bright and loves to learn new skills. He was fostered by Sarah and he has now matured into a wonderful companion who is much loved in his new home

Part Two
How to train your dog

This section contains an array of games and groundwork, bodywork and learning exercises that encourage your dog to use his senses, his body and his brain. The exercises are based on the structure that Marie has used in her training classes for over 20 years, and there are some added extras to give you plenty of choices in the way that you interact with your dog.

The exercises have been divided into several categories with certificates for completion (see p.39); this is for fun and not for competitive purposes. The aim is to work slowly through each category to motivate your dog to work with you, to activate his brain and to help him learn plenty of desirable behaviours in a way that is enjoyable for both of you. Ensure that he truly understands what you are asking him to do by taking your time, and avoid the temptation to rush in a bid to prove you have the smartest dog that ever walked the planet.

Incorporating jumps and other groundwork exercises into your training routine is fun for you and your dog. Here Jo and Monty are training on the beach

Getting started

There is not any specific time frame in which you should complete each exercise or section, although you should work with your dog on a regular basis to prevent him from becoming bored. Dogs enjoy being successful, just like us, and the more time you spend teaching your dog the faster his learning will become. Mental activity can be tiring and several short sessions throughout the day are far more beneficial than one long one. If your dog gets confused at any point, or loses interest, go back to an easier exercise and then give him a break or a relaxing TTouch bodywork session (see pp.35–38).

Be realistic

Dogs are smart and can be easily trained but they are also animals with their own thoughts, feelings, desires and drives. For some reason humans often expect dogs to be consistent, which is both unfair and unrealistic. Even a highly trained dog may not always perform on cue, and the politest dog in the world may suddenly develop an overwhelming urge to raid the trash. As dogs mature they go through many different phases, just like children, and even if you have established good recall with your puppy, he will probably start to ignore your requests as he reaches adolescence (between five months and two and a half years old). This is a normal part of his development.

While the following exercises will help you to raise a wonderful companion there will be times when you want to rip out your hair. Learn to differentiate between the feelings you have for your dog and any emotions triggered by his behaviour. Stay calm, stay engaged, be flexible and enjoy the journey.

Fluffy is tidying up her gardening kit. Dogs love to work, and games give them much needed mental stimulation

Verbal cues

It is up to you which words you use for sit, stay and so on. However, make sure they are clear and consistent and are not going to confuse your dog. If anyone else is looking after him or he needs to be rehomed in the future it is better to have taught verbal cues that other people are also likely to use.

Using a clicker and TTouch

To do the exercises in this book, it will help if you understand the principles of clicker training, Tellington TTouch training, and lure and reward training. They are all very good methods to help you clearly communicate with and train your dog so that you build an excellent bond. These techniques are introduced over the next few pages.

WHEN YOU NEED TO CORRECT YOUR DOG

Never resort to shouting, or threatening or hurting a dog. When understanding stops violence begins, and harsh reprimands are unpleasant, unnecessary and will have a detrimental effect on your relationship with your dog. Once he understands the boundaries and has learnt desirable responses, a firm word to tell him that he is behaving inappropriately, followed by praise (and a treat if necessary) the moment he stops the behaviour will be sufficient.

Important note
Flight, fight, freeze, 'faint' and fool around are five instinctive responses to stimuli. Many dogs go into freeze when confused, threatened or unsure, which may be misinterpreted by the owner or handler as disobedience or acceptance.

Clicker training

Clicker training is excellent because it quickly lets your dog know that he is learning correctly. It differs from lure and reward training in that the dog concentrates on learning the new behaviour, rather than just following a treat. The clicker is a small hand- or foot-operated device that makes a single clicking noise.

The click should never be used to gain the dog's attention; it is used precisely to mark a behaviour that you would like your dog to repeat, and there should be a short gap between the click and the delivery of a treat or reward for best effect. The click marks the end of that particular behaviour and your dog will soon learn that he needs to repeat it to encourage you to click and reward him again. An easy way to understand the method is to think of the 'click' as taking a photo of what the dog is doing at that moment in time. What would you like to see in the photograph? Not the rear end of your dog as he legs it out of the door with the Sunday roast in his jaws!

Introducing the clicker

Once you get the idea, clicker training is very straightforward. One of the ways you might begin is by 'luring' a new behaviour a few times so that the dog begins to get the idea and then waiting until he offers the behaviour before clicking. For example, if you are teaching your dog to sit, use food in your hand to lure the position, click as he sits and then reward. He will quickly learn to sit without the food lure.

Alternatively, you could click a behaviour that is naturally offered. For example, if your dog is in the habit of jumping up, click before his front feet lift off the ground and throw his reward on the floor. He will quickly learn that he gets no attention for jumping up but a nice reward for keeping all four feet on the floor.

CLICKER CUES

A cue or verbal label is not used until the dog has learned the new behaviour and is offering it consistently. If the cue is put in too quickly, a half-formed behaviour will be labelled and the dog's response to the cue will never be totally consistent. (See also Verbal cues, opposite.)

Mental activity can be tiring. Marie and Maisie take a break and enjoy a TTouch session

Coping with setbacks

Clicker training is great fun, especially if you take it slowly and make sure that your dog understands what you are asking. However, at some point, most dogs need to learn that you are not just a treat-dispensing machine and that they need to engage in the game to earn a click and treat. If your dog just looks at you, staring at your pocket or treat bag or even barking, put the treats into a pot or bag on a surface a few feet away so that he can see but not reach them. When he glances away from the treats – click, then get up and reward him from the treat stash. Repeat until he realizes that there is no point in watching the treats; he needs to focus and work with you so that you will be motivated to click and reward him.

Behaviours can be taught (or 'labelled') accidentally. Fluffy and Marie learned about clicker training together. A fine example of a cue mistake is that when Marie says, 'try again' Fluffy will bow. It's very clear to Fluffy as she heard that cue lots of times when she was trying to work something out and offered a bow. Marie thought she was teaching Fluffy something entirely different!

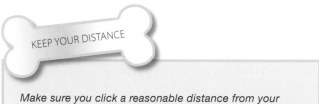

KEEP YOUR DISTANCE

Make sure you click a reasonable distance from your dog's head as it is noisy. Don't try it on yourself to see what it is like – honestly, it hurts like hell and your ear will ring for ages!

To start with, Sally follows a food lure when learning the sit

Layla is learning how to follow and touch the target stick

Tellington TTouches

If you have ever been told to avoid touching your dog in case you reward him for inappropriate behaviour, erase that from your memory right now. By using touch, TTouch gives beneficial information to the nervous system and can form an important part of a dog's education.

TTouch is a training system in its own right; it also blends well with other techniques. The groundwork and bodywork exercises add variety to training and improve balance, co-ordination and self-control. (For more information on TTouch, see p.141.)

A bodywrap (way 10) is also used to keep Layla a little more focused and the training game continues without the risk of bloodshed!

The benefits of TTouch are many. It helps to reduce unwanted behaviours including leash pulling, noise sensitivity and phobia, excessive barking and reactive behaviour towards humans and other animals. It reduces stress in dogs that live in kennels. Dogs that experience TTouch show a marked improvement in concontration and an increased willingness and ability to learn.

We have not yet met a dog that didn't like TTouch, but we have a high skill level because we have been using the technique for over 12 years. However, newcomers to TTouch can still achieve extraordinary results with relatively little knowledge. Never force the TTouches on your dog; if he dislikes the TTouches, check your technique or try using the back of your hand to move the skin. Alternatively, contact your local practitioner for help.

You can use the following TTouches alongside the training exercises and as an enjoyable way of connecting with your dog when you want to chill out together. When you have learnt them, and you and your dog are happy, take the time to teach them to other members of your family and friends.

HOW TO TRAIN YOUR DOG

SLOW OR FAST?

The speed with which you work will vary according to the dog's response and the situation. To calm a nervous or hyperactive dog and to promote relaxation and focus, work quite slowly. If your dog is unsure or tired, try working a little more quickly at the beginning.

Layla is a young terrier on foster from Battersea. She had developed an unpleasant habit of biting when overexcited. TTouch was an invaluable part of her rehabilitation process. Marie is using bodywork to calm an excitable Layla (top)

35

TTouch can give the nervous system valuable information

Orsa loves TTouch

Ear work

This is a lovely way of connecting with a dog: most owners naturally stroke their dog's ears anyhow.

1. With your dog sitting or standing calmly by your side hold his ear gently but firmly and stroke it from the base right out to the tip. If his ear hangs down, work in a downwards direction, and if he has upright ears, work from the base up to the tip.

2. Move the position of your hand each time you stroke to ensure that the whole ear is covered. Work gently but with intent. If you are too tentative you may make your dog nervous, particularly if he is a little ear-shy.

3. There is a 'shock point' on the tip of the ear, which can be worked by making circular movements with the finger and thumb. This is beneficial for dogs that have had a traumatic experience, have cold tips to their ears and/or are habitually nervous.

Ear work is a lovely way of connecting with your dog

You can use Clouded Leopard TTouches around the muzzle, as part of mouth work (see p.38)

Clouded Leopard

The TTouches break down into three groups: circles, slides and lifts. The Clouded Leopard is the foundation for all the circular TTouches.

TTouches work on the nervous system and therefore require relatively little pressure to be effective. To convey a sense of the amount of pressure that is appropriate when doing them, we use a system of numbers from one to ten. Place your thumb lightly on your cheek and rest your fingertips on your cheekbone. As lightly as possible, move the skin over your cheekbone without rubbing so that you can barely feel the bone. This is a one pressure. Repeat on your forearm, making sure that there is no indentation on the skin. Moving the skin over the cheekbone with a little more pressure so that you can just feel the bone gives you a three pressure. When using a three pressure on the forearm you should notice a slight indentation. Doubling the pressure gives a six pressure. Clouded Leopard TTouches are most commonly used with a pressure ranging from two to three, depending on the preference of the dog and the area on which you are working.

1. Visualize a watch face on your dog's body, make it about 1cm (½in) in diameter with six o'clock being the lowest point. With one hand lightly holding the leash, supporting the collar, or resting on your dog's body, place the fingers of your other hand at six on your imaginary watch face

2. With your fingers in a softly curved position, like a paw, push the skin around the clock clockwise, until you have made just one-and-a-quarter circles. Maintain an even

pressure all the way round, on past six until you reach eight. At eight, pause for a second and then move to another spot and repeat.

3. Ensure your fingers are gently pushing the skin rather than sliding over the hair. Check your dog is relaxed before moving on to another spot. You can do the Clouded Leopard TTouch over the whole dog, altering your hand position where necessary around the contours of the body.

4. Remember to breathe. Holding your breath stiffens your body and affects the TTouch.

ALTERNATIVE METHOD

If your dog dislikes this touch, try moving the skin in anti-clockwise circles or use light Zigzags instead (see p.38).

Among the many benefits of mouth work is its ability to relax your dog

Mouth work

Working around your dog's muzzle is an excellent way of helping him to learn. Mouth work helps to reduce excessive barking and oversensitivity and improves focus.

1. Stand beside your dog's shoulder or sit on a chair with your dog sitting down or standing, but importantly facing away from you. If he turns round to face you, stop immediately.

2. Support your dog's head with one hand and stroke his muzzle and sides of the face with the back of your other hand.

3. If your dog is nervous you can start by using a different texture such as a soft paintbrush or sheepskin mitt.

4. If your dog is happy, continue with a Clouded Leopard TTouch. Work around the jaw muscles and move the upper lip in a circular motion.

5. You can then slide a fingertip under the lip and rub it gently along the gum. Wet your fingers if the dog is dry in the mouth.

6. If your dog is happy, work both gums. Switch hands and work the other side of the mouth.

Zigzags

This is a great TTouch for warming up and cooling down your dog before and after energetic or competitive work. It can also be used for accessing areas on your dog's body that may be overly sensitive to contact.

1. Stand to the side of your dog – he can be standing or sitting. Rest your fingers on his shoulders and zigzag your hand along his back spreading your fingers apart as you move your hand away from you and drawing your fingers back together as your hand moves back towards you.

2. Keep the contact light but with enough pressure to ensure that you are not tickling.

3. Switch sides and repeat the exercise.

Zigzags improve body awareness and to relieve tension, tight muscles or fatigue. They are fantastic for dogs that go into freeze (see p.32) or those that lack hindquarter awareness

Introducing the ways

On the following pages (pp.40–139), you will find the exercises that will help you form the perfect partnership with your dog – or should we say more perfect than it is already. These have been divided up into several subsections, for fun and to make them more manageable. They do not have to be taught in any particular order – they are simply tips to ensure that you develop a great relationship with your dog from day one.

Establishing the basics

Beginning on p.40, these exercises teach your dog some of the most basic skills he needs to know. It is easy to fall into the trap of assuming that your dog automatically knows what you want or how he should respond, and many a dog has got into trouble for not being a mind reader (see also Don't make assumptions, p.26).

Bronze certificate

These exercises begin on p.52 and teach your dog some simple foundation exercises such as sit, come, off and down and include some fun games and practical groundwork exercises that will set you both on the path to a perfect partnership.

Silver certificate

The exercises in this section, which begins on p.101, are a step on from the important Bronze exercises and introduce stay, fetch and retrieve. They show you how to integrate other people into your dog's life in a way that is fun, safe and rewarding for all concerned.

Gold certificate

These exercises begin on p.117 and show you how to further your skills and provide ways to keep your dog mentally satisfied with more fun games, handy tips and training exercises, including the sit and down out of sight, chase recall, searching for hidden toys and treats and leg weaves.

Use an indoor kennel

1

There are many advantages to giving your puppy or dog his own safe space to settle for short periods of time. Aside from the obvious benefits for him when he is at home, at some time in his life he may need to be admitted to a veterinary centre and have to spend time in a recovery kennel. If he has been trained to settle in an indoor kennel, he is much less likely to be distressed by confinement at the vets.

If you go away from home with your dog, the indoor kennel or crate can be taken with you. It will provide somewhere familiar for your dog to settle. When staying with relatives you can be sure he will not cause a family rift by trashing their home if he is left unattended for short periods. Hotels and guest houses cannot allow dogs into their dining rooms and there will be a huge additional expense if he damages your room while you are eating – a crate will give you peace of mind so you can enjoy your meals. Leaving a dog in the car during the winter or summer months is not an option.

Children who live with dogs need boundaries too and can learn to stay away from the dog when he is resting in his kennel, whether the door is open or closed.

Use it wisely

Please bear in mind that while it is reasonable to expect a dog to sleep through the night in an indoor kennel, it is not appropriate to shut him in such a small space for long periods during the day. To become a happy and well-rounded individual it is vital that he is not isolated or confined like this. A dog should also see the indoor kennel as his safe space where good things happen, not a prison where he is dumped when his owner seems angry with him for some inexplicable reason (dogs don't always understand our logic, see pp.12–13).

Ensure that he always has access to water when he is in his crate.

Crate training helps to keep puppies safe. A yummy bone or stuffed Kong™ in your dog's den is a much better alternative to chewing on electrical cables

Cookie has settled in her crate and is munching happily

When your dog is getting tired, encourage him into the kennel but leave the door ajar

Introducing the indoor kennel

1. Place your dog's bed or bedding in the crate or kennel and feed him some of his meals in it too. When your dog has been active and is becoming tired, encourage him into the kennel with a stuffed Kong™ or chew toy but leave the door ajar. At this stage the only place you should give him exciting things to chew is in the indoor kennel.

2. When your dog is happy to go into the kennel, begin to close the door to confine him for short periods. Make sure he has something to chew on.

For reluctant dogs

1. If your dog really seems to hate the kennel and won't go in even for his dinner, put a small amount of really tasty food into his food bowl and place the bowl in the kennel. Close the door to keep him out.

2. When he is desperate to get in to the food just open the door, make no attempt to close the door behind him.

3. Repeat until your dog is happy to go in and out of the kennel and confident enough to settle down with a chew or toy. It should then be possible to close the door for short periods, if necessary.

Cookie is just desperate to get in to those treats!

Related ideas…    **2   7   11**

2 Provide effective housetraining

Housetraining is not rocket science and can be quickly achieved if you are observant and ensure that your hound is actually taken outside when he needs to toilet. Dogs are creatures of habit and can not only to trained to go to a certain part of the garden to do the necessary, but also to empty on cue, which can be really useful, especially when you are away from home.

Puppies usually need to relieve themselves when they wake up, after they have eaten and after (or during) an energetic game. Watch for signs of circling or sniffing. Quickly and calmly take him outside and stay neutral so you don't distract him. Give a tasty reward when your pup toilets in the right place. When he begins to understand why he has been taken out, attach a cue word (see p.32) quietly as he is relieving himself.

The more times you can reward a puppy for going in the right place, the quicker housetraining will progress and he will learn to ask to go outside. If you have adopted an older dog that is housetrained remember he doesn't automatically know where *you* want him to toilet. Take him out to his toileting area frequently and reward him for going in the right place.

Understanding accidents

If there is an accident, accept the blame and be more observant in future. If you tell the puppy off it may confuse him into thinking that the act of toileting rather than the location has upset you. And this may encourage him to find a good hiding place to toilet (behind the settee) or, worse, to clean up his own mess.

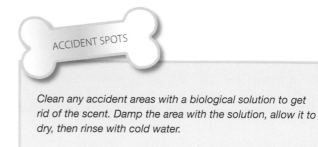

ACCIDENT SPOTS

Clean any accident areas with a biological solution to get rid of the scent. Damp the area with the solution, allow it to dry, then rinse with cold water.

ON BEHALF OF YOUR DOG

If the weather is foul, please don't just shove your dog out of the door, and then be surprised if he sits on the doorstep crying pathetically. When you relent and let him indoors he will probably promptly leave you an unwanted present. He is not bad – he didn't know what he was supposed to do. Be brave, put your coat on and help him out until he understands about housetraining!

Make sure that you give your dog plenty of opportunities to toilet outside

Related ideas... **1** **7** **8**

Follow a sensible feeding regime

3

It is up to you to decide when, where and what your dog is going to be fed. Remember dogs do what is rewarding for them. They can be really appealing and cute when they are trying to obtain an early dinner but if you inadvertently reward your boy for being pushy, and feed him when he asks, you can hardly blame him for leaping about and squeaking because he thinks that his dinner is far more important than that long-distance call from a much-loved relative.

Choose when and what to feed your dog but be aware that certain foods can trigger unwanted behaviours in some dogs

Setting standards

Decide on a good diet, put the food down and leave it for 10 minutes. If there is anything left in the bowl, clear it away and do not offer anything else until the next mealtime. Fussy eating habits tend to develop very quickly if you constantly offer alternatives.

Don't feed your dog from your own plate while you are still eating. If you do, do not be surprised when you feel a cascade of drool down your legs when eating, or worse still, catch sight of a lovely trail of saliva on your visitors during a barbeque or dinner party.

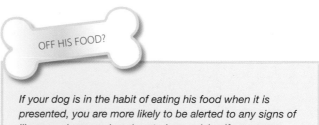

OFF HIS FOOD?

If your dog is in the habit of eating his food when it is presented, you are more likely to be alerted to any signs of illness and can seek early veterinary advice if necessary.

Related ideas...

4   **5**   **6**

4 Cultivate good food bowl manners

Dogs need to learn how to be polite and confident around both food and the food bowl and this can be done in a kind and motivational way using clicker training (pp.33–34).

1. Put a little food into the bowl and hold it at chest height. Your dog may rush forward to look up at the bowl: say nothing and when he steps back click and treat. Be patient and repeat until he learns to step back a few paces.

2. The next stage is to start lowering the bowl towards the floor. If he dashes forward, say nothing, raise the bowl again, wait for him to back off then click and treat. Repeat until your dog learns to step back and you can get the bowl nearer and nearer the ground. If you have already taught the 'off' cue (see way 14) it can be used at this stage. Stay patient and repeat the process until your dog learns to keep back while the bowl is placed on the floor.

Cookie gets a high-value reward from Marie for politely backing away from the bowl and sitting

Naomi helps to extend food bowl training. Cookie has learned 'off' so here Naomi gives the cue and pauses to help Cookie build self-control before she releases her to the food bowl

Related ideas... 3 5 6

Teach food bowl confidence

It is very sad that new owners are still frequently advised to take the dog's food bowl away while he is eating 'to prove who is the boss'. In reality this is more likely to stress a dog and cause him to develop a condition called IBS (Irritable Bowl Syndrome). The dog is actually inadvertently trained to growl and guard both the food and the bowl because a human near the food bowl means a potential threat to his meal.

Naomi helps Cookie to understand that it is rewarding for a human to be near her food bowl while she is eating

Be fair to your dog

Let's face it, many humans would swiftly develop FFJS (Fast Fork Jab Syndrome) if some clown kept attempting to snatch their plate away just as they were tucking into a tasty meal, so it is important to encourage your dog to feel confident about humans being near his food bowl while he is eating. A simple and effective way to do this is to add tasty tidbits to the bowl while your dog is eating. It is then potentially rewarding for people to be near the food bowl. On the very rare occasion that you may need to remove the bowl when your dog is eating, you will not have a problem.

This exercise will have the added benefit of teaching your dog to behave appropriately with food around other dogs

Related ideas...  3   4   6

45

6 Ensure appropriate eating from the hand

Many dogs learn to grab food from the hand, which is both unpleasant and painful. It makes good sense to teach your dog how to be confident and gentle when taking food offered by hand; even if he has already learned the art of snatch and grab, you can still teach him better manners using this exercise.

Ouch! Cookie grabs for a treat!

When you offer the reward, keep it trapped under your thumb

1. With palm facing up, trap a piece of food under your thumb and offer it to your dog.

2. If your dog tries to grab it, keep your hand and especially your thumb very still and release it only when he slows down and softens his mouth to take it.

STOP MOUTHING

If your dog mouths your clothing or hands the second he gets wind of a treat, teach him the 'off' exercise – way 14.

Cookie learns that the only way to get the food is to calm down and be gentle

Related ideas...   7   14   21

Use effective rewards

Different dogs value rewards in different ways. Some love to work for food, while others prefer to work for a game with a specific toy; some may enjoy both equally. And then, of course, there is also verbal praise and physical contact.

Grade the value of treats that you give to your dog. For example, he may come to you for a biscuit when you call him in your home but when there are other distractions outside you may need to give him a higher value reward, such as a tiny bit of his favourite food. The same applies to toys. Find out which of his toys your dog rates the highest and vary the toys you use when working with him to keep him interested.

The most important thing to remember is that a reward needs to be just that – a real reward for the dog, and therefore must be appropriate for the environment that he is in at the time and for the precise momont that you want him to respond.

Give your dog regular mealtimes (see way 2), then the additional tasty treats that you offer will become more valuable. A few special toys that only come out when you play together and that are put away while your dog is still keen to continue with the game will become more highly prized than that old smelly chewed thing that has been quietly rotting in the flowerbed through the winter.

RATION REWARDS

Don't always have food available and all his toys around so your dog can help himself when he wants. If he can do this, he is less likely to be excited by food or toy rewards. If he has constant access to everything why would he be motivated to work to earn them?

Your dog may not come to you for a biscuit when there are other distractions…

…If this is the case you will need a higher value reward (don't panic we aren't really suggesting you buy a chunk of beef)

Related ideas…　　　6　8　9

8 Train your voice

Dogs have a very acute sense of hearing and can pick up a variety of pitches and sounds. Like people, they respond well to praise and an interesting, well-paced speech pattern. They will be far more engaged and keener to learn if the person that is working with them uses their voice effectively.

You can even practise encouraging your dog to respond to a whisper somewhere quiet. You may be amazed at how even a dog with 'deafness' can become more switched on and focused if you vary the way you communicate with him verbally. Timing is also important. When you give an oral cue, allow him a moment to hear and understand your request and then respond accordingly.

Many owners fall in to the trap of either talking too much or not praising enough when teaching their dog new skills. A weak, flat or monotone voice, or gruff, short commands will do little to motivate your dog and a terse attitude can cause a dog to withdraw and become aloof or depressed. At the other end of the scale, a permanently excited, squeaky high-pitched voice can over-arouse or confuse a dog.

Facial expressions naturally follow the cadence of the voice, and boring intonation equals a very dull and uninspiring teacher. Even if your dog or puppy is deaf (see p.29) you can still use your voice to praise and encourage him as he will learn to read your body language and respond to your facial movements.

Be positive

It is far more pleasant for both you and your dog if you use positive words rather than negative terms and let him know how you do want him to behave rather than focusing on the unwanted behaviour. For example if he is being noisy, it is clearer to the dog if you ask him to 'be quiet' rather than shouting 'don't bark!' Your mind will have clear image of your dog being peaceful as opposed to seeing the continuing behaviour.

SILENCE PLEASE

If you are training a new behaviour with the clicker, remember not to talk or add a verbal cue until the dog has fully understood what you are asking him to do.

Physical contact and soft words of praise are highly appreciated

Related ideas... 6 7 9

Work on your posture and hand signals

Dogs communicate primarily with body language so it is often easier for them to learn visual cues, which can then be paired with verbal cues. Be clear in your own mind about the hand signals you intend to use and please do not keep them a secret from anybody else who lives with or cares for your dog.

Be aware of your own posture. For example, leaning forward from the waist when you call your dog, and staying in that position as he approaches might cause him to curve away or hang back. Your body language will appear challenging and he is trying to appease you. Sadly, this in turn can look as if he is being deliberately naughty and refusing to come when called. As a result some people start escalating their own behaviour, which will worry the dog even more.

Marie uses arm signals to recall Oz and Maisie

If you have called your dog and he is reluctant to come to you and looks very concerned, defuse his anxiety by half turning away; this will trigger him to come to your side. In contrast if your dog always approaches at high speed and kneecaps you on arrival, it might help to take a quick step towards him to slow his pace when he's a few yards out.

When training your dog by encouraging him to use his initiative and perform a behaviour of his own free will, (free-shaping) it can be helpful if you sit. This way you are less likely to lean or shuffle or involuntarily give clues; all of which may distract him. It also helps him to know the only 'clues or hints' he will get will come with your clicks and treats as he works towards the goal behaviour.

Sally works out how to target the mat as Marie sits patiently waiting to click and treat

RECALL IN THE DARK

If you are a long way from your dog in fading light, stand tall and use your arms to help him to locate you.

ESTABLISHING THE BASICS

Related ideas...   7   8   15

49

10 Use bodywraps and T-shirts

This is not about dressing up your dog as a fashion accessory. Both bodywraps and T-shirts have practical uses and can provide an important first step for service puppies that go into freeze (see p.32) when they first wear a puppy coat or body harness, and for dogs that are noise-sensitive. We hope we don't need to remind you that it is really important that you refrain from laughing at your dog when he is wearing a T-shirt or bodywrap. Body wraps and T-shirts can be bought on the internet (see p.141).

Putting a T-shirt or bodywrap on a timid dog can help him to feel less shy and can help a bouncy dog to settle and become focused on what he is being asked to do. They can also help dogs to overcome a fear of being contained or touched. Giving a dog sensory input with T-shirts or a stretchy elastic bodywrap can also help to reduce over excitability when travelling in a car (see also ways 29 and 30). You can use the bodywrap if your dog is worried about wearing a seat belt or a regular harness. He may feel safer having something around his body that moves as he breathes, and the harness or seatbelt can be popped on over the top of the wrap once he feels confident.

When wearing a bodywrap, Layla finds it easier to concentrate on the job she has been asked to do

T-shirts can give a dog a greater sense of security

CONFIDENCE BOOSTER

Try using a bodywrap if your dog is nervous about being approached by other dogs when out and about. It will not only help his confidence but might also encourage other owners to keep their own dogs under control as they will think your dog is recovering from some strange condition!

Put the middle of the wrap around your dog's chest

Cross the wrap under your dog and bring both ends up over the ribcage

Tie the knot to one side and let the puppy move around

Putting on the wrap

1. Approach your dog calmly with the wrap, If he is worried about the wrap, stroke it gently against his side or do some circular TTouches (p.37) with the wrap in your hand.

2. When he is happy, place the middle of the wrap across your dog's chest and bring the wrap up and over the top of his shoulders.

3. Cross the wrap over his withers and take it round the ribs and under his sternum.

4. Cross the wrap under your dog and bring both ends up over the ribcage.

5. Tie the ends in a bow or a quick-release knot. Make sure that the knot or bow is off to one side of the spine and that there is plenty of give in the material. The idea is to give him sensory input, not to truss him up in a strait jacket.

6. Now encourage your dog to move around to stop him from going into freeze (see p.32). Play a game or give him some treats if he tries to chew the T-shirt or wrap.

ALTERNATIVE TIE

If your dog is worried by the sensation of the wrap crossing underneath his body, tie the wrap in a figure of eight instead.

Related ideas...   **1**   **11**   **12**

51

Bronze Certificate

Bronze Certificate – key skills

These exercises deal with problems such as jumping up, running away with toys (or your best shoes), sensitivity to contact, poor recall, and so on, which are not just associated with puppies. With consistent training and an understanding approach you can teach your dog to behave more appropriately and to enjoy being touched.

The Bronze exercises are instrumental in building a strong foundation on which further training will be based. If your dog or puppy cannot perform the exercises in this section you are unlikely to be able to teach him the more advanced games and exercises in the Silver and Gold sections.

Games & groundwork

Starting on p.77, the games and the groundwork exercises feature the Dog Spinny and Dog Twister, two games that encourage you to interact with your dog. They are particularly useful if you have not been able to spend much time with your dog during the day and can be used to increase bonding and reduce boredom.

The other exercises in this section are groundwork exercises, which help you to teach your dog to negotiate the type of obstacles he might encounter when out on a walk. Dogs that are only used to walking in a park may be thrown if they are asked to find their way over different obstacles in new situations.

Successful socializing

These exercises begin on p.81 and build on previous exercises. You can intersperse them with the earlier exercises, as it is paramount that your dog gets out and about as much as possible. But be realistic, if you have not taught him to accept a collar and walk on the leash, a trip to a busy town is unlikely to be a success, and if you have not formed a good bond with your dog, he is unlikely to pay much attention to you in an exciting park!

Important skills

These exercises begin on p.89 and are all useful for increasing the variety of skills your dog possesses and for helping him to cope with some of the more difficult aspects of living with humans.

---

100 Ways to Train the Perfect Dog

Bronze Certificate

This is to certify that

Owner: _____ & Dog: _____

Have successfully completed training to become a perfect dog [and owner!] Well Done!

Sarah and Marie

Practise calm containment

Puppies are naturally wriggly and need to be taught how to settle and be still without inadvertently alarming them. Of the pups labelled 'difficult' that we have worked with, many were probably frightened by someone using heavy handling techniques. These puppies would have switched into panic mode and learnt to snap at hands put near to hold or restrain them. They were not being dominant: they were afraid.

As the puppy gains confidence in your handling skills, you can begin to teach him to accept restraint but this must not be rushed. This important exercise has far-reaching benefits – children or even adults may be compelled to throw their arms around your dog and hug him. Hopefully you will be able to teach your friends how to approach dog respectfully so this unlikely to happen, but it is better to be safe than sorry. The exercise is also a useful foundation skill if you want to put a harness on your dog.

Here's how it's done

1. Kneel on the floor and sit back on your heels. Place the puppy between your knees and thighs with him facing away from you to reduce the chances of him jumping up at your face.

2. Put your heels together to form a V-shape so that the puppy cannot reverse.

3. Keep your arms relaxed and place your open palms lightly on the pup's chest.

4. Go with his movement: if he tries to walk forward, gently draw him back to you, keeping your hands relaxed, and contain him in the original position. The aim is to create a mobile barrier, not to pin him to one spot.

5. Some dogs accept this very quickly but others continue to wriggle. Stay calm and keep repeating the gentle containing movement until your dog relaxes and is happy to sit quietly with you.

You only need to contain the puppy for a few moments before you let him move freely around the room or garden. If he jumps out of your arms and starts playing with your hands, re-direct the play behaviour onto a suitable toy. Repeat this exercise a few times and keep the session short, talking quietly using long, low syllables to induce calm.

Keeping your hands soft, cup the puppy gently around the chest

Containing the older, bouncy dog

Run your hands gently over the dog's body to see if he is concerned by contact around his hindquarters. If he is worried about being touched here you may need to use TTouches (pp.35–38) to help him overcome this fear.

1. Stand up and support your dog around his hip between your calves (and knees if he is large).

2. Position your heels together so that they touch.

3. Keep your knees and hips soft and avoid squeezing the dog tightly between your legs.

You need enough connection through your legs so that he cannot wriggle free but is not alarmed by being contained in this way.

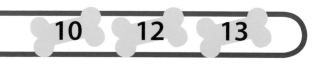

Related ideas…   **10**   **12**   **13**

12 Work on all-over handling

Teaching your dog to accept and enjoy contact is an important part of his development. It enables you to make regular health checks, to handle him without causing upset, trim toe nails, groom him, treat minor cuts and grazes, clean muddy paws, towel dry him and so on. If *you* are unable to touch your dog, it is highly unlikely that he will let anyone else near him either, and attempts to stroke or handle him when he is in a confined area will probably result in defensive behaviours.

BRONZE CERTIFICATE – KEY SKILLS

TTouches can be used to accustom your puppy to contact all over his body

Monty is wary about being touched by people he does not know, so Jo starts by working with him on her own

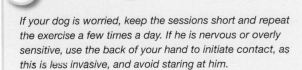

REDUCE WORRY AND NERVES

If your dog is worried, keep the sessions short and repeat the exercise a few times a day. If he is nervous or overly sensitive, use the back of your hand to initiate contact, as this is less invasive, and avoid staring at him.

1. Start by containing your dog or sitting next to him.

2. Run your hand lightly and slowly over his body without applying too much pressure. Use the Clouded Leopard TTouch (p.37) to help keep him calm and to show him that contact is something that is truly pleasurable.

3. If your dog is wary about contact around his hindquarters, for example, start by working on another area and use the light Zigzag (p.38) to access the pelvic region. You can also use this technique for helping him to be less sensitive to having his paws handled.

4. Use different textures so that your dog becomes accustomed to lots of different sensations and does not develop a fear of being groomed (see way 50).

Be aware

Dogs that are hand-shy usually lack confidence or carry tension through some part of the body. They may also be sensitive to noise and overly aroused by movement.

The Clouded Leopard TTouch helps Monty to realize that contact is nothing to worry about

Related ideas… 10 11 13

Teach your puppy to accept the collar

It pays dividends to teach your puppy to wear a soft, light collar, harness and leash as early as possible (see also pp.20–21).

1. Prepare his nervous system for having something around the neck and shoulders by working around the collar area, ribs and upper part of his back by using TTouches (pp.35–38).

2. Put the collar and/or harness on for short periods and feed the puppy or play a game with him so that he realizes he can still move around and that the equipment is nothing to be concerned about.

3. Once the puppy has accepted the collar, attach a light leash with small, light clip onto the ring and allow him to move about with the leash attached.

4. If he tries to chew the leash, engage the puppy with a toy or tidbit. If he is still determined to chew the leash, use TTouches to accustom him to being handled around the mouth and teach him the 'off' or 'leave' cue (see way 14).

CHANGE HIS FOCUS

If your puppy writhes around when you attempt to put on the collar or attach a leash, squeeze some soft cheese or pâté on to the door of a refrigerator or washing machine to change his focus.

Attach a light leash with a small clip onto the ring and allow your puppy to move about with the leash attached

Related ideas…   **10**   **11**   **12**

Teach the 'off' or 'leave' cue

It is never too early to start teaching a dog 'off' or 'leave'. This is a very important skill as there is nothing more irritating than a dog that bounces around jumping up at people or grabbing anything in his path. Your dog will quickly learn that this cue means he must remove his teeth or feet from whatever has taken his interest, which may include your favourite shoes, his leash, your hand, or the dining table, laden with the fruits of your culinary labours. It can also be used to stop your dog scavenging when out and about.

Allow your dog to take the treat you are offering – as long as he is gentle

1. Hold a treat between your finger and thumb. Offer it to your dog with the palm of your hand facing up and allow him to take it gently. Repeat this a few times. Say nothing at all.

2. Offer another treat and as your dog moves forward to take it, turn your hand over and close your fist, making sure that your thumb is tucked inside. He will probably push at your hand, or he may paw it, but ignore this behaviour. Keep your hand still and refrain from speaking to him or reprimanding him in any way.

3. The moment your dog stops trying to gain access to the tidbit, turn your hand over, palm up and give him the treat.

4. Repeat this process a number of times, making sure that you give more treats than you withhold. Remember to stay quiet.

If your dog pushes or paws at your hand simply ignore this behaviour

Add a verbal cue

Most dogs quickly understand that a closed fist means that there is not any access to the food and that there is little point in pushing and pawing at the hand for the treat.

Once your dog is consistent with this behaviour, put in a quiet verbal cue. As you make a fist and turn your hand over to withhold the food, say whatever word you want to use. Make sure it is a word you feel comfortable with but not one you have used previously with an inconsistent response. Some people use 'off' as it is descriptive and it is unlikely to have been used before, while others use 'leave'. Be patient, and avoid the temptation to add the verbal cue before your dog fully understands the required behaviour.

Cookie backs off and sits politely waiting for her treat. What a smart Cookie!

TOY TIME

Extend the exercise by practising with toys. Initially, it is more effective to use items that allow you to turn your hand over and give the visual closed fist cue, like this toy on a rope.

Related ideas…   4   6   15

15 Introduce appropriate greetings

Many dogs get over-excited and jump up when meeting people because they have not been taught how to greet appropriately. The problem is made worse because people greet dogs in different ways, which can be really confusing, especially for a youngster.

We cannot educate the entire population how to greet our dogs appropriately but we can teach our dog that this action by a human can be quite rewarding.

The following steps show how to follow the hand touch through to a greeting behaviour that is rewarding and acceptable to both humans and dogs. The hand touch is also a brilliant way to introduce the clicker (see pp.33–34).

1. Offer the back of your hand to your dog. Have your fingers pointing downwards and hold the clicker in the other hand well away from his head. When his nose gently touches your hand, click, pause a couple of seconds and then give a small soft treat.

2. Make gentle eye contact (half-close your eyes) and then offer your hand. Click when your dog touches it and, as before, give a small treat.

3. Repeat step 2 a few times, increasingly making more direct eye contact until your dog is confident.

4. Gradually lean and move more quickly towards your dog until he accepts this approach by immediately touching the front of your hand.

5. As your dog gains confidence, begin to involve other people in training this behaviour, talking them through the

Marie turns her hand over and gives Cookie a small soft treat

exercise. He should greet them with a hand touch and then turn back to you.

6. Finally, when your dog is offering this behaviour consistently as a greeting, put in a verbal cue, such as 'say hello'.

Don't train your dog to be a mugger

To avoid your dog mugging strangers for treats, ask people not to give your dog treats from their pocket. If somebody wants to give your dog a treat and you feel awkward about saying no, hand your treat pouch to them.

Cookie is learning to touch the back of a hand gently with her nose

Naomi joins in and Cookie is learning to greet her in the same way

Related ideas...   6   7   9

Teach a calm 'sit'

Believe it or not many dogs have never learnt to sit on cue. This is a really important skill to teach your dog, and the clicker makes it effortless. You do not need to wrestle your dog into a sit position by pushing his hindquarters to the ground, and even young puppies can learn to sit in a few sessions.

Before you begin

Make sure the floor is not too slippery: your dog may find it difficult to maintain the position if his front legs are slowly sliding forward on your lovely polished floor. Dogs with docked tails may also find it hard, depending on the length of the tail, and a nervous dog may also be a little reticent to sit. Use the TTouches (pp.35–38) to help release tension through the back and hindquarters. You can also try the bodywrap to give him more body awareness (see way 10).

Teaching the sit

1. Hold a small tasty treat near your dog's nose with your fingers curved and pointing upwards; this forms the basis of the hand signal.

2. Slowly raise your hand at a slight angle so the dog follows with his nose and begins to tip his head back; click and treat.

3. Repeat steps 1 and 2 and click when the dog is almost sitting.

4. Repeat step 3, but this time wait until his bottom actually touches the ground before you click and treat. Your dog is now responding to an upward hand signal.

5. When the dog is consistently responding to the hand signal introduce a word cue by saying 'sit' as you give the signal. Click and treat.

Once he understands both the verbal signal and the hand signal you will no longer need to use the clicker for this exercise.

Hold a tasty treat and slowly raise your hand so that the dog follows it with his nose...

...click when he puts his bottom on the floor, then give him the treat

Related ideas...   **11**   **17**   **24**

Give lessons in 'down'

As well as being a useful exercise to teach your dog in terms of obedience, 'down' is also important as it is the basis for asking your dog to settle after an exciting game, when visitors come to your home or when you take him into a new environment. It is also useful for teaching dogs to lie down when travelling in a car crate, as they will often feel safer and will be less aroused by outside stimuli when lying down.

Begin in sit

1. Most dogs find it easier to learn the down from a sit position (see way 16). Hold a small tasty treat near your dog's nose, with curved fingers pointing downwards; this will form the basis of the hand signal.

2. Slowly lower the treat in a straight line towards the floor.

When your dog follows your hand with his nose, click and put the food on the floor

Lower the hand with the treat in it to the floor in a straight line

3. As your dog begins to follow your hand with his nose, click and after a few seconds drop the treat between his paws. This will encourage him to get into the habit of looking to the floor for the treat, which will diminish the chances of him learning to do 'doggy press-ups' and following your hand back up in search of another treat.

4. Again from the 'sit' position, take the treat lower so that this time the dog's nose is close to the floor and his front legs begin to bend. Click and after a few seconds drop the treat.

5. Still from the sit, lower the treat from nose to floor and then slowly push it back towards his chest.

6. Wait until he drops his whole body into the 'down' position then click and after a few seconds drop the treat between his paws.

Push the food slowy back towards his chest to encourage 'down'

When he drops his whole body down, click and drop the treat between his paws

7. Repeat this a few times until the dog gets the idea. Then try lowering your hand, giving the same hand signal towards the floor.

8. Click when he takes the down position and after a few seconds drop a treat.

Once your dog has understood the exercise and takes up the down position from the sit, lure him from 'stand' to 'down'. Click and drop the treat as before.

When your dog is consistently offering down from sit and stand, say 'down' as you begin to give the hand signal. When he understands the verbal cue, the clicker has done it's job and is no longer needed for the down.

An alternative is to sit on the floor. Bend one leg so that there is just enough room for your dog to lie down and lure him underneath so he takes up the down position.

GIVE YOUR DOG A HINT

If your dog remains standing remember that he does not automatically know what you want him to do. It is natural for some dogs to stand as they follow the food down. Lure him back to a sit and try again. If this still does not work try lowering the food to the floor and slowly draw it forward.

Still not working?

He may have poor awareness of his hind legs and/or be carrying a lot of tension in that area. Doing some TTouches (see pp.35–38) along the back, around the base of the tail and hind legs can really help to bring awareness to those areas and make it easier for your dog to consciously move into the 'down'.

Lure your dog underneath your bent knee so he has to take up the down position

Related ideas…  7 16 28

Play a shared game

This exercise teaches your dog that a shared game is safe and good fun. If he does not learn to share a game with you, he will probably start to play the natural doggy possession game; that is standing a couple of paces away from you and grabbing the toy whenever you try to pick it up, which can be frustrating. Puppies need to learn how to play appropriately as soon as possible but older dogs can also be taught this exercise.

1. Start with your dog on a flat collar, or harness, and trailing leash. Choose a toy that is big enough for you both to hold. Wiggle the toy along the ground and encourage your dog to mouth it. When he takes the toy, stroke him, praise him and have lots of fun.

2. While you are both holding the toy, stroke your dog but quietly pick up the end of the leash before you release the toy so that your dog cannot bounce away with it.

3. When your dog is happy to share the game and to give up the toy when you ask for it using the 'off' or 'leave' cue (see way 14), start to throw the toy a short distance, but leave the leash trailing so that you can contain the game.

Marie prevents Layla from bouncing away by picking up the leash before releasing the toy

Layla wears a collar and leash so that Marie can contain the game

Layla is learning to release the toy

Retaining control of the game

Avoid staring at your dog as he comes back towards you with the toy as this can trigger a doggy tease and chase game. Call him and turn away. When he is close to you, quietly step on the trailing leash so he can't bounce away. Stroke him and have fun without touching the toy or making eye contact. You want him to feel confident and happy around you with the toy in his mouth.

Related ideas... 4 9 19

Introduce the fun retrieve

Puppies and young dogs will pick up things they should not have because they naturally explore with their mouths. A young dog will rapidly form the idea that a fantastic game can be had if he grabs something that he knows will make humans chase him. He will very quickly learn that this can be a great attention-seeking device.

Puppies use their mouths to understand and learn about their world

1. If he helps himself to something, regardless of what has been taken, quell your desire to scream or pursue your dog; simply call him.

2. Run in the opposite direction if necessary (sob quietly if you need to cry). This will trigger him to follow you.

3. Praise your dog calmly on his arrival at your side, and trade by inviting him to have a game with one of his own toys. He will learn that he gains your attention and has more fun playing with articles that he is allowed.

Encouraging play

If you have a dog that doesn't seem interested in toys, you can encourage him by working through the following sequence:

1. Put a toy on the ground and when your dog looks at it, click and treat. Repeat this a couple of times.

2. When your dog looks at and then begins to move towards the toy, click and treat. Repeat a couple of times.

3. Wait until your dog moves forward and touches the toy. Click and treat and repeat so that your dog understands the game.

4. Continue to slowly shape the behaviour until your dog is picking up the toy.

5. Once he has grasped the idea that you want him to pick up the toy, call him to you as he picks it up and turn away to encourage him to come to you. If he drops the toy, encourage him to go and pick it up again.

Run in the opposite direction if necessary – this will trigger your dog to follow you

Related ideas...   **7**   **8**   **9**   **20**

Teach the recall

The recall is a serious exercise. A good recall means that you can let your dog off the leash safely. To be really effective it needs to be rewarding and fun for your dog, so it is a good idea to keep back part of his daily food ration and repeat the recall many times every day.

BRONZE CERTIFICATE – KEY SKILLS

Recall is very important

1. Start at home where there are few distractions. Every time you remember that you have a dog, call his name and say 'come'. Have your hand in front of you holding a tasty treat and draw him towards you. Make sure you are standing or sitting upright as this will encourage him to come closer; if you lean forward he will probably hang back (see way 15).

As your dog approaches, let him scent the food and raise your hand

Call your dog by his name and add the word 'come'

2. As he arrives let him scent the food you have in your hand. Raise your hand slowly so that as he lifts his nose to follow it, he will sit. Give the reward. Use calm, verbal praise and avoid high pitched tones.

3. Talk to and touch your dog and on some recalls give a small piece of food every few seconds. It is essential he learns that it is worth while staying with you, rather than simply grabbing a treat and running off.

Call his name and say 'this way' so that your dog gets into the habit of watching and following you, rather than expecting you to follow him

Introducing changes

Once your dog understands the game, vary the type and timing of the rewards. Establish a good recall at home before expecting him to return from exciting smells or other dogs when out and about.

Clip the leash on and off so that he learns to accept this quietly in controlled conditions at home. It is very irritating if your dog bounces away every time you try to clip his leash on in the park. When you start to let your dog off-leash in the park, choose a quiet time with few distractions.

Recall lots of times, reward (remember to vary the reward), and sometimes clip the leash on and walk a few yards or use a little ear work and the Clouded Leopard TTouches (p.37) so that he stays with you once the leash is on, and then release him again.

Avoid taking the same route around the exercise area and putting the leash on to go home at exactly the same point. Most recalls should mean a game, fuss, treats or freedom again, not leash on and home.

Clip on the leash and walk a few yards, then release your dog again

WHEN RECALL GOES OUT THE WINDOW

Some breeds have been selectively bred for their scenting ability and others for their sight for the chase. When these natural and very strong instincts are aroused (at the park, say) some dogs seem genuinely not to hear the human voice. The good news is that they do respond very well to a whistle, see way 22.

Related ideas...  **7**   **8**   **9**

Start line training for recall

A dog is a creature of habit, so you can train him to stay within a certain range by using a long line. A flexi-leash is useful for giving your dog additional freedom of movement when he must be on a leash, but because there is always a degree of tension on a flexi-leash, it is not suitable for using to teach a recall response.

Use a long line to train your dog to stay within a certain range

Remember to click as he begins to follow, and treat him too

Making a start

If possible, use a padded or cotton line as this is kinder on your hands. With a rope or nylon line, wear gloves to avoid burns if your dog shoots away. Attach the training line to a static H-shaped or step-in dog harness. Don't attach it to your dog's collar or a stop-pull harness as he may suffer a neck injury if he suddenly reaches the end of the line.

1. Attach the line to your dog's harness and let him go. As soon as he passes you or moves too far away, but well before he reaches the end of the line, call 'this way' and change direction so that you are moving away from him.

2. Use the clicker to help him to understand this exercise. Click as he turns and begins to follow. He will continue towards you to get his treat. Remember you are not clicking to gain his attention but to mark that he had already changed direction and started moving towards you. This is the behaviour that you want him to repeat.

Drop the line and repeat the work – only using it as a fallback

3. When your dog is consistently changing direction to follow you, drop the line and allow it to drag on the ground.

Practise in different exercise areas until your dog learns to keep a watchful eye on you and follow you each time you change direction. When this is established you will no longer need the clicker or the long line for this exercise.

Related ideas...   **7**   **8**   **9**   **20**   **22**

Introduce recall with a whistle

Whistle training is excellent if a dog tends to get lost in the exciting scents or sights he finds outside. The noise of a whistle seems to be able to cut through any distraction and gain a dog's attention. However, your dog needs to strongly associate coming to you when he hears the whistle.

Naomi blows the whistle and gives Cookie a portion of food

1. Split your dog's meal into five or six portions. He should already be with you as he knows it is his supper time. Blow the whistle and give him one portion of food in his bowl. Blow the whistle again and give him the second portion and continue until all the food is given. Repeat this exercise over a few meals.

2. Your dog should now be strongly associating the whistle with the food and you can start using the whistle to recall him from anywhere in the house and garden. You may notice that on arrival he is already salivating in anticipation of a yummy reward. Blow the whistle and give him some really tasty treats when he comes and practise this exercise on and off throughout the day.

3. Once the association with the whistle and food has been strongly formed you can try taking the whistle to the park – choose a quiet time when there are few distractions – to build his confidence and consistency.

Always reward his responses

When your dog understands recall with a whistle, it is important to give the high value treats only for a high value recall. If he is lazy in his response, thank him for arriving but withhold the food or give a bland food reward.

Never tell him off for a slow response or it will put him off coming when called in future.

BRONZE CERTIFICATE – KEY SKILLS

AVOIDING BAD HABITS

If your dog ignores the recall, don't wait until this becomes a bad habit. Go back a few steps and reinforce your training until you get a solid and consistent response again.

Related ideas...  **7   20   21**

23 Coach appropriate behaviour for greeting children

Dogs need to learn how to approach children calmly without bumping into them, jumping up or knocking them over. This can be overwhelming and frightening for small children. Most children love to be involved with training the family dog. Parents can help both the dog and child to get things safe and right.

1. This exercise is best done with two adults and a child. One adult holds the dog on a collar and leash about 1m (3–4ft) away. Make sure that the dog cannot rush forward to make contact with the child. Another adult stands behind the child to quietly coach and give support.

2. As the adult holding the dog allows him to move towards the child, encourage the child to throw a tasty treat on the floor, at least 30cm (1ft) in front of them. This will distract the dog from rushing.

3. Repeat until the dog begins to look for the treat on the floor, rather than rush right up to the child.

4. Increase the distance slightly and have the dog move towards the child again. The child's supporting adult should help to time the treat throwing, so that it gets the dog's attention as he approaches. Gradually build up the distance so that the dog develops the habit of stopping short of a child, rather than running right in and mugging them.

Even a friendly and well meaning dog can be scary when he is much bigger than you are

It can be very frightening for a child if an excitable dog rushes up to them

The dog will learn to slow down and approach children appropriately

Related ideas... 6 15 20

Ask your dog to follow a hand target

Now that your dog has learned to touch the back of a hand in greeting (way 15) you can extend this exercise to teach him to hand target and follow. This is an easy exercise to teach and very beneficial as you will be able to ask your dog to move without pulling on his collar or leash. It also forms the basis for working off-leash.

24

1. With your dog watching you, move your hand a centimetre or so (2in) and as he begins to follow it with his nose, click and treat. The treats can be delivered from the hand or dropped to the floor.

2. Gradually extend the distance and time that your dog will follow your hand. Teach him to follow both hands.

3. You can now encourage your dog to follow a hand while walking by your side to gain his attention when he becomes distracted.

OWNERS OF SMALL DOGS

If you have a small dog you can use a target stick instead of your hand to protect your back from injury due to constant bending.

Cookie is learning to follow Marie's hand. As well as being a practical exercise, this also gives Cookie a more appropriate way of responding to hand movement instead of the biting that she was doing before

In potentially distracting situations, use hand targetting to encourage your dog to follow you

Related ideas...   **6   9   14**

25 Teach walking on a leash

A dog's natural movement is usually much faster than human walking pace so unless you teach your dog to walk slowly and in balance he may find it difficult to walk without leaning into the leash.

BRONZE CERTIFICATE – KEY SKILLS

Dogs are not machines. They can easily lose focus and balance when excited by the environment or a new distraction and thus rush forward to the end of their leash. If the owner rewards by following it is hardly surprising that the dog drops all his weight into the leash and drags them along; it takes two to maintain a pull.

1. With your dog on a short leash, stand still and take a step back with the leg nearest to him. Use your hand target skills (way 24) to encourage your dog to come back to you and do a U-turn in the direction of the leg you have dropped back.

Marie takes a step back and encourages Cookie to do a U-turn

Dogs can easily out-walk a human (top) so Sarah uses a clicker to teach Cookie to slow down and focus on her (above)

2. Move your leg forward again. Click and treat as the dog moves into the correct position.

Marie clicks when Cookie is in the correct position and rewards her

3. Keep his attention by asking him to hand target until the distraction has passed. The ultimate aim is to teach your dog to be relaxed and confident enough to be able to walk with you on a loose leash.

USE A DOUBLE-CLIPPED HARNESS

Until your dog is skilled at loose leash walking you may find it helpful to use a double-clipped leash attached to a harness and flat collar, or the balance leash (see way 26).

Related ideas... 13 18 21 22

Lead from both sides

Some dogs are so habituated to being led from their owner's left side that it totally throws them if a person has to lead or even handle them from the opposite side. Even if your dog is young, he may still be confused if you ask him to walk on your right side. However, if you have been practising your hand target exercises it should be an effortless exercise (well for him anyhow). This is a great opportunity to practise some groundwork (such as ways 34–36, 73 and 74) as it will give him something to focus on.

26

The exercise may take longer to teach if you are the one that has been habituated to leading your dog from one side, so work slowly if necessary to minimize the chances of you tripping over your dog and squashing him flat. It pays for you both to have learnt this exercise when you are taking your dog out and about in a busy town or if you want to progress to the child leading exercise (see way 68).

The steps are the same for the on-lead exercise, way 25, but, of course, you will have your dog on your right-hand side.

Teaching your dog to be comfortable being led from either side can be beneficial if you are walking along a busy road or need to switch sides to avoid an oncoming bouncy dog (or a cat!)

Related ideas...   **24**   **25**

71

27 Make use of a target mat

A target mat is a great tool for shaping behaviour and teaching your dog to work away from you. It is also a bridge to teaching your dog to settle down in different locations both at home and in a new environment. You will need a small piece of bedding, carpet or flat plastic.

BRONZE CERTIFICATE – KEY SKILLS

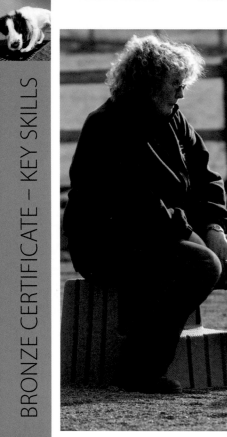

When your dog looks towards the target...

1. Put the mat on the ground near your dog. Sit on a step or a chair nearby. When your dog looks towards the mat, click and throw a treat to the other side of the target.

2. As the dog moves back towards you having retrieved the treat and either looks at or touches the target, click and throw another treat over the target.

...click and throw a treat to the other side

As your dog touches or looks at the target, click and throw a treat

3. Repeat this step until the penny drops and your dog understands that the click is linked to him interacting with the target.

4. The next stage is to pause for a few seconds as he stands touching the target then click and treat. Repeat this step a few times.

5. You can then withhold the click as your dog touches the target to see if he will offer a sit or down. Only ask for 'sit' or 'down', if your dog is well practised at these and offers the positions consistently on a single word cue, otherwise you will confuse him.

TIMING

To extend the time that he will stand, sit or down on the target, delay the click for a few seconds at a time.

Try withholding the click as he touches the target to see if he will offer a sit or a down

Related ideas...   16   17   27

28 Introduce 'stand' on cue

Teaching a dog to stand on cue is useful for several reasons. It enables you to groom, bath or towel-dry your dog without him sitting, wriggling or dropping to the floor. It also enables you to teach him a controlled exit from a car or house and to wait calmly and patiently while you put on his harness, collar, coat or that rather fetching doggy T-shirt you just purchased.

Encourage your dog to stand, click and throw a treat on the floor away from you. When he returns to you, click while he is still standing and throw another treat. At some point he may sit or lie down but just wait patiently until he stands again then click and throw the treat.

Alternatively try standing sideways on to your dog and lure him into a stand position with your fingers curved sideways away from him. This will form the basis of a hand signal. Take care with your hand height: if you hold it too high he is likely to sit, if you hold it too low he may lie down. When he is in position click and treat.

Practise this exercise over a few sessions. When your dog is consistently offering the stand attach a cue or command.

When your dog is consistently offering the stand, attach a cue or command

The ability to ask your dog to stand on cue comes in useful for a variety of reasons, such as for grooming

Related ideas...   16   17   27

Practise safe travel in a car

Take your dog out in a vehicle as soon as you can. Begin by going on short drives that end in a lovely walk so he associates cars with something pleasant. Boring drives or visits to the vets do little for the dog–car bonding process. To keep your dog safe when he is travelling, he needs to be on the back seat with a specially designed dog seatbelt that attaches to the human seatbelt, or in a custom-made car crate in the back.

29

Make sure that he has been able to relieve himself before he gets in the car and avoid feeding him prior to travel to limit the chances of carsickness. If he is an anxious traveller, use TTouch ear work (p.36) and a bodywrap to help him feel more secure.

Inka wearing her seatbelt

Related ideas...   **10**   **16**   **17**   **30**

BRONZE CERTIFICATE – KEY SKILLS

30

Work on controlled exits

It can be entertaining to watch people opening their car door at the park and either wrestle with their dog while they put on a leash or be knocked sideways as he barges his way to freedom. It is not so amusing when it happens to you, and there will also be occasions where you need to open the car door but do not want him to get out.

Use a clicker and hand signals to ask him to sit or to lie down so that he learns to listen to you and wait calmly for you to get him ready.

1. Ask your dog to sit or stand when you open the door.

2. Clip on his leash and ask him to wait using a hand signal so that he learns not to leap out the moment you step back from the car.

3. Ask him to jump down or lift him if he is small and ask him to sit or stand by the side of the car.

You can click and treat him so that he really understands what you expect of him and use TTouches (pp.35–38) around his head to maintain his focus. Enjoy your walk!

Ask your dog to wait for a moment instead of leaping out the moment you open your door

Related ideas...   **9**   **25**   **29**

31 Discover searching for food

This is an easy, peasy skill to teach and it will form the basis for finding hidden toys and treats later. If you have had a hectic day and have not had time to work with your dog, you can use this exercise to encourage him to hunt for his supper, which will give him the opportunity to use his nose and his brain. It is also helpful for dogs that are over-the-top when they greet their owners, as it shifts the focus from the person to the treats.

1. Simply scatter some food or treats around you while your dog is watching.

2. Use the cue 'find' as your dog is sniffing around.

Extend the exercise by scattering the food further away from you.

Once your dog understands the 'find' cue, scatter the food in an accessible place without him seeing. Fetch him and walk to where the food is spread; give him the 'find' cue to encourage him to search on his own. He should learn that 'find' means he looks for the food on the ground, not watch your hand to see where you are going to throw the food.

To begin with allow your dog to watch as you scatter the treats

Related ideas…   18   24   27

Bronze Certificate

Yahoooooo! Well done. You have taught your dog some very important foundation exercises. Photocopy the Bronze Certificate (on p.52) and stick it on your fridge to remind both you and your dog what you have achieved together. Keep up the good work and progress to the next stages of training. There are plenty more games and skills to learn before you start the Silver Certificate, but for now reward yourself and your dog for mastering the vital lessons that form the basis for everything to come.

Play with the Spinny

No, this is not something that involves you whizzing your dog around in circles while he is attached to a rope or leash by his teeth! It is one game in a really cool range of interactive dog toys developed by trainer Nina Ottosson (see p.21); they are designed to be used indoors or outside. The dog spinny is perfect for beginners and puppies.

32

The Spinny is just one of many interactive dog games developed by Nina Ottosson

1. Load the spinny by hiding some treats in the holes underneath the rotating wooden disc. Swivel the disc to show your dog how to access the first treat. Your dog will quickly learn by watching you that he has to rotate the disc with either his nose or his paw to find the hidden treats. Sit back and see if he can find the other treats on his own.

2. Encourage your dog by praising him when he starts to touch and then move the disc. Once he has found all the tidbits, refill the spinny and start again. If he loses interest in the toy, use more exciting and higher-value treats or put the game away and get it out another time.

Important note
Always stay with the dog while he is playing with this toy and do not allow him to chew or gnaw on the wood.

Archie has learnt to push the swivelling disc around with his nose to find the treat concealed inside

Related ideas...   **7**   **18**   **27**   **32**

33 Introduce the Dog Twister

This is another Nina Ottosson interactive dog game that encourages the dog to use his paws to access the treats. Go through the same steps as with the Spinny (way 32) and show your dog how to win his reward. He will probably learn in a relatively short space of time that he can move the blocks in each direction with his paws.

Some dogs are more naturally inclined to explore with their paws. This fun game encourages them to use their paws in a positive way as opposed to digging through your newly planted flower pots. It also teaches your dog to alternate between using his right and left paw, which will help him to be less one sided.

Sally is using her paws to move the blocks

Related ideas...   7   18   27

34 Work over low-level poles

Groundwork helps to improve focus and co-ordination, and gives you the opportunity to practise the hand target exercise (way 24). The ground poles form the basis for jumping over obstacles later on. Start by working with your dog or puppy on a harness and flat collar. Once he understands the exercise, try working off-leash.

1. Lay a series of poles flat on the ground.

2. Ask your dog to sit in front of the poles and then ask him forward with a hand signal.

Increasing the difficulty

If he is happy with this exercise, you can raise the ends of the poles by placing them on small blocks. Increase the difficulty by raising some poles higher than others or raising alternate ends.

Be realistic and do not raise the poles too high in the early stages and keep the sessions short.

Encourage your dog forward with your hand and remember to give him a reward

Related ideas...   7   9   13   24   25

Create confidence using the low-level walk-over board

Teaching a dog to walk over a raised board will help him learn to negotiate steps and to feel confident about being on a table when at the vet or groomer. It is also a nice starting exercise for dogs that may go on to compete in agility, and a good opportunity to practise the 'sit', 'stand' and 'down' positions.

You can create a walk-over board by placing a wide plank of wood on low crates, or make a more permanent structure if you are lucky enough to have some DIY skills. Make sure that the board is securely fixed and will not wobble – your dog must feel safe when walking over the apparatus.

How it's done

Start with your dog on a harness, flat collar and double clipped leash. A nervous dog may be reluctant to leave the ground on cue, so begin with the board on the floor if necessary.

Do not drag your dog over the board. Let him work it out in his own time, using the hand target exercise (way 24) to show him what you want him to do. Eventually you can ask him to stand or to sit on the board and use TTouches (pp.35–38) to give him the experience of being handled when off the ground.

Finally, if he is happy and you are in a safe space, ask him to walk over the board off-leash.

Cookie is learning to walk over a raised board. This adds variety to training and teaches her to feel confident when standing on a raised platform

Using TTouches gives Cookie the experience of being handled when off the ground

GAMES & GROUNDWORK

Related ideas...  12 24 25

36 Introduce negotiating slippery surfaces safely

Teaching a dog to walk over a variety of surfaces improves his confidence and co-ordination and encourages him to think about where he is placing his paws through the different textures he will feel on his pads. Many dogs are challenged if they are faced with a slippery floor, particularly if they are old or stiff through the hindquarters.

1. Lay a line of plastic mats or add a combination of different textures such as car mats, blankets and wood in a straight line in your home or in your garden.

2. Put a harness on your dog and attach one end of a double-clipped leash to the flat collar. Attach the second clip to the harness. If your dog is calm when walking on a leash you will not need a harness.

3. Walk your dog over the different surfaces and watch his responses.

WORK WITH TTOUCHES

If your dog is hesitant use the Clouded Leopard TTouch (p.37) and bodywrap (way 10) to give him better mind–body awareness.

Inka demonstrates perfect walking on shiny surfaces. Different textures help to improve focus and co-ordination

Related ideas...  24 25 35

Find an appropriate training class

37

Some owners are reluctant to attend training classes because they have an ingrained image of an uptight (usually middle-aged), control-freak of a trainer who barks out orders and whose favourite words are 'Don't', 'Never' and 'No'.

Fortunately things have progressed in the training world. There are now more choices for people who want to work with their dogs in forward-thinking, positive ways, and the divide between those who train their dogs for competitive purposes and those that just want a family friend who comes when he is called is becoming narrower.

Training classes are a great way to socialize and train your dog in a controlled environment and give you the opportunity to meet other owners with dogs of a similar age. Do your research before you sign up for the classes and ask if you can sit in and observe a training session before you attend with your dog. If the trainer will not let you check out the classes, find another one. Watch and listen to everything that is going on in the class. Are the owners being encouraged and engaged and talked to? Or are they being talked at and made to feel stupid? Does everyone (including the dogs) look happy? Is the trainer clear in what he/she says and does? Is everything under control or is it total chaos? Talk to other owners once the class is finished. Finally, before deciding to attend, go with your gut feeling.

In short, avoid large crowded classes and those where there is a lot of noise and/or shouting. Stay well away from anyone who pushes and pulls the dogs into position, squirts water at the dog, and uses sound aversion, choke chains, prong collars and other negative techniques.

Positive training techniques develop trust

Related ideas... 8 9 13

38 Go happily out and about

A change of environment is important for your dog's wellbeing. Sadly, many dogs are almost permanently confined to the back yard, which means that they miss out on the essential stimulation of new sights and smells. Even a drive in the car in the company of his favourite human can be fun and rewarding for your dog.

Oz and Maisie enjoying a country walk

The more places you can take your young dog the better. Remember to take your treat pouch, toys and clicker, and practise your skills in a variety of situations. Give him the chance to experience as many new things as possible. Obviously you need to ensure that you have good recall, and recall with distraction, before you even consider letting your dog off-leash in any public place. It is amazing how even a Slow-Mobile-Dog can get up to near breathtaking speeds when on the trail of a deer, or someone else's picnic lunch.

Cookie is learning how to negotiate steps

Related ideas...   20   22   34

39 Stroll about town

Walking along a noisy, busy street amid lots of legs and rustling carrier bags can be pretty mindblowing for a dog. You will need to have taught your dog to be led from either side (way 26) so that you can switch your position to keep him away from the road as necessary.

This is where your skills as a trainer really come in, as your dog will no doubt attract a lot of attention. The hand-touch greeting, hand follow and sit are probably the three most important exercises the dog-about-town needs to know. You will also be thrilled that you taught the 'off' cue, if your walk takes you past any rubbish on the pavement.

Oz is calm and happy in town

Related ideas...   14   15   16   24   26

Take a hike in the country

There can be few better things in life than a country walk in the company of a faithful hound. Not only are you both enjoying the freedom of a lovely stroll but you have an opportunity to practise your training skills in a new environment.

40

Cookie learns about bridges

You can incorporate some groundwork into your walk and take advantage of the varied terrain, gates, bridges and stiles to teach your dog how to negotiate his way through, around, under and over obstacles. Dogs that are not very body aware or are nervous may be unsure about uneven ground or clambering through wooden fencing, for example, but you can help them to improve their co-ordination and confidence by setting up some simple obstacles at home.

Naomi and Orsa enjoy a walk in the country

Related ideas...   **34**   **35**   **36**

Ensure polite meetings with adults and children

41

If you have taught your dog the appropriate greeting exercise he should already know how to say hello to his admirers. Keep your treat pouch on hand so that you can ask him to touch their hand and then turn to you for his reward. Make sure that he keeps all four paws on the ground – don't allow him to jump up at small children.

Adults and children need to follow some simple rules too. Ask them not to feed your dog and only let them stroke him if he is calmly in a sit or, at the very least, has all four feet on the ground. Encourage them to stand slightly to the side and slowly stroke his chest. Explain that he will be calmer if he can see their hand and that if they try to stroke the top of his head or the back of his neck that he will naturally look up to see where their hand has gone.

Dogs must be calm and well-behaved when meeting other people, especially children. Orsa is a star

Related ideas...   **6**   **15**   **23**

42 Walk in the park

Footballs and children and bikes oh my! Footballs and children and bikes OH MY!! Parks provide plenty of stimulation and lots of distraction. There is usually a whole heap of activities going on and it is a fantastic place to take a young dog to broaden his life experience.

It can be very helpful to take a young dog out in the company of well-behaved older dogs

This is Cookie's first visit to the park and Marie continues with her training. Despite lots of distractions Cookie is behaving impeccably

When your dog is nervous

If your dog is nervous or has not had the opportunity to socialize, keep him on a leash and stay at the edge of the park. He will be able to see everything, but you will have an escape route if he is overwhelmed.

Ask a friend who has an older or more confident dog to accompany you. Dogs learn from watching the responses of other dogs but make sure your friend's dog knows how to behave appropriately.

Use the ear work and Clouded Leopard TTouches (pp.35–36) to help keep him calm. If he can work and take a treat, ask him to do a few simple things, such as sit or down, to shift his focus, but bear in mind, if he is really afraid he will not be able to sit or eat. He is not being dominant – he is scared. He may find it easier to be on the move so ask him to follow your hand (see way 24). Keep the visit short and gradually build up his confidence, interspersing visits to the park with activities that are less of a concern.

Parks provide plenty of stimulation. Maisie is watching the swans quietly and calmly

KEEP AWAY

Unless you are in an on-leash only exercise park you will no doubt have several dogs coming up to greet the new guy. Not every owner will be as responsible as you, so if you see a dog approaching in a not-so-friendly manner, get your dog's attention and then use this tip from our lovely friend and fellow TTouch practitioner, Billie Machell. Shout as loudly as you can (without freaking out your own pooch) 'My dog has a highly contagious skin condition!' It works!

If he is totally over-aroused, try to walk him in an S-shape to encourage bend through his body, and use ear work to lower his heart rate and respiration. Try to get his attention by using the exercises you have practised in a quiet environment. If his behaviour escalates take him back home and go back a few steps in his training.

Related ideas...   15   16   17   20

Teach sensible behaviour around livestock

43

Any meeting with other animals needs to be calm and controlled. Chasing or lunging and barking at cats, wildlife, farm animals and so on is not acceptable. The earlier you introduce your dog to a variety of other animals the better, as it can be very hard to change the behaviour of a dog that has already learnt to chase and/ or kill another animal.

1. Keep your dog on a leash, and use a steady voice to keep him calm.

2. Ask him to sit quietly and watch the animals from a distance; use the clicker and treats to reward his appropriate behaviour. Ask him to turn and look at you before you allow him to meet the other animals.

3. Use TTouches (pp.35–38) to give him sensory input and to help him to stay settled.

Your dog should be calm and quiet when meeting other animals. Cookie is meeting Poppy, a miniature Mediterranean donkey, and is sitting beautifully

Related ideas...   14   15   16   38

Calmly meet other dogs

44

In general, dogs know what to do when they meet strange dogs and use their complex and subtle body language. They will often sniff the ground to acknowledge the presence of another dog. They may also curve slightly away as they move towards each other, sit and/or turn around if the other dog seems agitated or worried.

Unfortunately, if our dog is on the leash we often interfere with the natural communication process and unwittingly trigger conflicting signals by shortening the leash and holding it tightly for example. This may be a common reaction but it causes the dog to brace, which changes his posture. It also prevents him from using his body language effectively. If a dog is approaching you head-on along a pathway, try to leave enough space between the dogs so that they can signal to each other without being able to lunge at one another.

Be sensible and be fair

Please understand that some owners keep their dogs on the leash for a good reason and that they are making every effort to keep their dog under control in a public place. They have a right to have an enjoyable walk without your over-friendly pooch ruining their day.

If other owners also have their friendly dogs off-leash and are happy for them to play together, your dog will have a fantastic time and will soon build up a wonderful group

Sniffing the ground together is a good sign that the dogs are getting on and do not feel threatened by each other

of doggy friends. To prevent him developing over-excited barking behaviour on the end of the leash every time he sees another dog, teach him how to walk quietly on the leash with his new friends.

Remember to play with your dog too. He will happily accept that you decide when he can play with other dogs and that you are not just a taxi to an exciting social event.

Related ideas...   **20**   **25**   **26**   **37**

Meet skateboards and strollers and bicycles

45

Cookie is behaving beautifully. She is getting plenty of opportunities to see and hear lots of different things

Objects that move quickly can trigger a dog to chase, and revolving wheels can be rather exciting for a young dog. While this is a natural response, it does not have to become an automatic reaction.

Use meeting moving objects as a training opportunity and ask your dog to sit calmly while skateboarders, cyclists and so on go past, and also teach him to walk quietly alongside, behind or in front of moving objects.

Related ideas...   **38**   **39**   **41**   **42**

Practise calmness while watching exciting activities

There will be times when a young dog is very aroused by watching an exciting, noisy activity. As well as using your clicker, TTouch and verbal praise, you can create a 'balance leash' to prevent him from pulling into his collar, which will add to his frustration.

Young dogs can be excited by some activities

SUCCESSFUL SOCIALIZING

1. If your dog is on your left side, hold the leash near his collar in your left hand and hold the end in your right hand. Take the length of the leash behind his left elbow and bring it up diagonally between his front legs. Take it across the front of his right shoulder and thread it up through his collar.

2. Hold the leash in both hands and gently draw your lunging hound back by giving him an ask-and-release signal on the chest with it. Ask is a gentle pull, and release is how it sounds.

3. Stay relaxed in your shoulders and arms. A tight hold on the leash will encourage your dog to pull more. The sensation of the leash across the chest is really helpful in settling an exuberant dog and it helps to draw back his centre of gravity.

4. Hold both parts of the leash in your one hand and use your other hand to do some TTouches (pp.34–38) to keep him engaged with you.

You can also use TTouches to help keep him calm

Related ideas...   **37**   **38**   **43**   **45**

47

Enjoy watching the world go by

Take time on your walk to sit down and simply watch the world go by. This simple exercise teaches your dog to be patient and provides him with an effortless time out from an exciting game in the park.

Find a bench or a patch of grass and sit quietly with your dog. Use ear work, Clouded Leopard TTouches and zigzags (pp.35–38) to help him to stay engaged with you while watching other people and dogs pass by. You can also use the clicker and treats to regain his attention. Gradually build up the length of time you can both sit quietly like this.

Watching the world go by teaches patience and is a great opportunity to use the TTouches

Related ideas...   10   38   39   41   42

48

Make practise visits to the vet

Every dog will go to the vet at some point, but the clinic does not always have to be associated with something unpleasant. Some vets encourage young dogs to come in and meet the staff so that they can become familiar with the smells and sounds. Even if your vet does not offer this sensible opportunity to socialize your dog, you can still make the experience as enjoyable as possible.

Not only will it help him to stay calm it is also less stressful for the other clients (both animal and human) if your dog is able to sit quietly, so take your clicker and treat bag along. Remember you can also use TTouches (pp.35–38) to keep him settled.

The balance leash (see way 46) will help him to keep four paws on the ground, while the hand target exercise (way 22) is brilliant in this situation as it enables you to direct your dog without having to haul him around by his collar. A T-shirt may also keep him calm (see way 10).

Cookie has called at the vet's clinic for a social visit. She is meeting the staff and learning how to behave in the reception area

Related ideas...   39   41   42   44

Introduce mops and brooms

49

Most puppies will see mops, brooms and vacuum cleaners as huge moving toys. Unless we make it more rewarding for them to do something else, they will want to chase them.

To help your dog understand that there are some things that he cannot play with, teach the exercise below and repeat the steps if necessary. Start by holding the mop or broom still or keeping the vacuum cleaner switched off. Then progress to moving the broom, mop and so on.

1. With your dog out of the room, scatter 10 tasty treats on the floor, hold the mop (or other item) and let the dog into the kitchen. He will go to the treats, and as he approaches each one click before he reaches it to mark the behaviour.

2. Let your dog see you throw another treat on the floor away from both you and the mop. As his eyes turn to follow the treat, click to mark him looking away. Repeat a couple of times.

3. Wait until he looks away from you and the mop, click and throw the treat. Repeat a couple of times.

4. Wait until he actually moves away from you and the mop. Click and treat.

Any moving object, even a mop, can excite a young dog

GIVE A JACKPOT

As a special reward for excellent behaviour, click and give a jackpot of treats (that is several all in one go).

Cookie moves towards the treats that Marie has thrown on the floor (left) and has soon learnt to move away from the mop (above)

Related ideas...   **14**   **31**   **46**

50 Make grooming a pleasant experience

Grooming should be pleasant for both you and your dog. It strengthens the bond between you, and keeps your dog's coat and skin healthy by improving circulation and removing dead hair. Avoid being too vigorous and watch your dog's expression to ensure he is enjoying the experience, not simply politely waiting for you to stop.

Grooming helps to develop a bond between you and your dog

Young dogs are often wriggly when they are groomed and may mouth the brush or start playing with your hand. If you have already taught him the containment and handling exercises (ways 11 and 12), it is unlikely that this will be because he is over-sensitive to contact and is more likely to be because it is a new sensation. Put some squeezy cheese or doggy pâté on the fridge door to take his mind off the brush.

If your dog is nervous or unsure, use a sheepskin mitt or a soft Jelly Scrubber™, which will make the grooming experience less challenging and therefore possibly more pleasurable. Use TTouches (pp.35–38) to access areas that may be of concern to your dog.

If your dog has serious concerns about being groomed, take him to the vet for a thorough health check as he may have problems with his neck, back and/or hips. If he is given a clean bill of health, contact your nearest TTouch Practitioner who will be able to teach you bodywork exercises that will help your dog.

A soft Jelly Scrubber™ (left) or a sheepskin mitt (above) are good alternatives to a brush, if your dog is sensitive

Related ideas...  11 12 16

Trim nails without stress

Dogs develop problems with nail trimming for a number of reasons: they may have been hurt by having too much nail removed, resulting in the sensitive quick being clipped; the owner may have inadvertently gripped the paw, which can panic a dog; they are nervous about the noise of the clippers; or they were not accustomed to having their feet handled in early puppyhood.

Make clipping enjoyable

1. Supporting his paw gently – avoid holding on for dear life – start by using TTouches (pp.35–38) on his feet and also around his nails. Circle one of his front paws on the front of the other front leg if he is worried about having his paws touched.

2. Stroke his paws with the clippers.

3. Hold a matchstick or small twig near his paws and clip the piece of wood to help him become accustomed to the noise of the clippers.

4. Clip the nail on a slight angle and exhale as you clip to prevent yourself from holding your breath, which will make your grip tighter.

TAKE TOO LITTLE

If in doubt, remove less nail than you need to. It is far better to clip his nails regularly than to take off too much nail, which may hurt him.

Working gently around the nails and toes helps to overcome concern about having the feet handled

IF HE'S TICKLISH

If he has ticklish paws use a soft artist's watercolour brush around his feet to reduce his sensitivity before you touch his feet with your hands.

Work around his feet with TTouches

Related ideas...   **11**   **12**   **25**

It is well worth teaching your dog to accept a muzzle as part of his training. Even the most placid dog might bite if he is in pain and has to have treatment at the vet's. If he is used to and comfortable wearing a muzzle, there will be one less area of stress for you, your dog and your vet.

IMPORTANT SKILLS

Putting on a muzzle does not have to be something negative or unpleasant. Vets usually have a range of muzzles that are cleaned after every use, but it will be more pleasant for your dog to wear one that bears his own scent. It can therefore be worthwhile to invest in a basket muzzle that fits him perfectly.

Preparation work

If you think your dog is likely to be very wary of a muzzle begin by using TTouches around his face. A soft wrap, placed gently around his muzzle and tied loosely around the back of his neck is another good starting point.

Breaking down the exercise to its simplest form by using a piece of soft elastic around the muzzle and head will help build confidence and trust

You can use a length of soft elastic – simply pop it over his nose, cross it under his jaw and then tie both ends together in a bow behind his ears. Ensure it is not too tight. If he slips it off with a paw, calmly pop it on again and give him a treat or play a game to distract him.

1. Place the muzzle on the ground and when your dog looks at it click and treat. Repeat a couple of times.

Spend a few moments to do some TTouches around the muzzle area

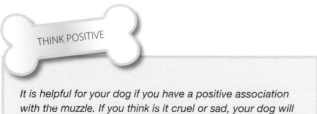

THINK POSITIVE

It is helpful for your dog if you have a positive association with the muzzle. If you think is it cruel or sad, your dog will pick up on your feelings and respond accordingly.

With encouragement your dog will start to move towards the muzzle

Given time your dog will happily take a treat from the muzzle

Gently hold the straps behind your dog's ears

2. Wait until your dog begins to move towards the muzzle, click and treat.

3. Place a treat just inside the muzzle and click as your dog leans forward to eat it. Repeat until your dog is confidently taking the treat from inside the muzzle.

4. Hold the muzzle in your hand with a treat near the straps, click as your dog takes the treat. Repeat a couple of times.

5. Progress slowly, moving the treat down the muzzle until you are able to post a treat through the hole in the end of

the muzzle and your dog is confident enough to put his nose inside to take the tidbit.

6. Gently hold the straps behind your dog's ears as he takes the treat.

If he panics and tries to shake off the muzzle, withhold the treat and allow him to shake free. Be patient, and give him time to advance and retreat until he is prepared to take the treat out of the muzzle repeatedly and allow you to hold the straps behind his ears gently. When he is confident with the straps behind his ears, the muzzle can be secured. Keep distracting your dog with tidbits so that he becomes used to the feel of it.

Remember to put the muzzle on at home and feed tasty treats so that it is associated with pleasant experiences for your dog. If your dog usually has to be muzzled at the vet, put his muzzle before going inside so that he enters as confidently and as calmly as possible.

Post a treat through the hole in the muzzle

TEMPTATIONS TO AVOID

• *Do not make any attempt to correct your dog verbally or hold the muzzle on forcibly. He will quickly learn to accept the slight restriction in order to get the treat, so please be patient.*

• *Do not do up the straps until he is entirely comfortable with putting his nose into the muzzle.*

Related ideas…   **10**   **11**   **12**   **48**

53

Habituate him to loud noises

Some dogs are more sensitive to noise than others, but sensitivity does not have to develop into a phobia that will affect them for the rest of their lives.

As dogs learn from people and animals around them, it is really important that you are totally neutral when your puppy or young dog hears his first fireworks, heavy rainfall, thunder and so on. If you look or sound upset, your dog will quickly learn that loud noises are frightening. If you leap about trying to excite him intending to make him think loud noises are fun, you might also alarm him. Stay calm and feed him treats or play one of your usual games so he associates something pleasant with loud noises.

Tracey uses TTouches around Cuillin's hindquarters and he is totally at ease as a huge truck rushes past

If he does become concerned, pop a bodywrap or T-shirt on him and use ear work and Clouded Leopard TTouches (pp.36–37) if he will sit by you. If he needs to retreat to his indoor kennel, allow him to, but make sure that it is not placed somewhere that will make the noise louder. Cover his kennel with a blanket and leave the door open so that he does not feel trapped. Play the radio, draw the curtains and stick to your usual routine.

Noise sensitivity is usually associated with tension through the hindquarters so you can use the Clouded Leopard TTouches to release tension around his lower back, hips, tail and hind legs. Even old dogs with serious concerns about noise have been helped through the use of TTouch.

T-shirts or bodywraps can help your dog become more confident with household noises, traffic or thunder and fireworks

NOISE PRACTICE

You can purchase CDs to help your dog become used to a variety of noises (see p.141). Avoid the temptation to put your shiny new CD on full blast before reading the instructions that come with it. The guide will tell you how to use the CD to help rather than traumatize your dog.

Related ideas... 10 11 39 45 46

Teach the 'exercise finished' cue

54

Up to this point ,the sound of the clicker has marked the end of an exercise. However, as each task is refined and cues are added, you also need to have a visual and verbal cue to let your dog know when the game or exercise is over.

We use a light shoulder touch and a verbal 'OK'. Choose anything that works for you and be consistent. Use it to end each exercise.

Marie uses a light touch on the shoulder to let Cookie know that the exercise is finished

Related ideas... 7 8 14 46

Introduce 'settle down'

55

All dogs need to learn how to settle down, whether in their own home, when visiting friends or relatives, on the bus or train or in the vet's waiting room.

If you have worked through the Bronze Certificate section your dog will already know how to target a mat (way 27). Now extend this training by using the same method to teach him to respond to a cue by settling into a 'down' on a small piece of mat or bedding. Gradually extend the time that he is expected to settle and make it more rewarding by giving him something like a stuffed Kong™ to chew on.

Settle anywhere

When he has learned to settle at home, make sure that you also train the behaviour in several different locations, using the same piece of mat or bedding to help him make the connection. When he understands what is required attach a verbal cue to the behaviour.

Use the target mat training to teach your dog to settle down on a mat or bedding

Related ideas... 28 38 46

Teach calm 'hiding'

A dog can become over-excited or fearful of fast-moving objects, other animals or other dogs that approach quickly and directly towards him, especially if he is on the leash. If you are on a narrow path, such as a canal towpath, it is not always possible to move out of the way (unless you and your dog fancy a swim!). However, you can teach your dog to hide behind you on cue.

IMPORTANT SKILLS

By teaching him how to hide behind you, you let your dog know that you are going to keep him safe, so he will not feel he has to bark and lunge to protect himself. It also teaches him self-control, and that it is much more rewarding to move behind you if things get over-exciting.

Making a start

Teach this exercise away from narrow paths and fast moving objects to begin with.

Cookie moves behind Marie as a bike passes and gets a reward

1. With your dog on the leash at your side, encourage him to target the hand on the side nearest to him. Click and treat.

2. Step back on the leg that is nearest to him and move the hand on this side slightly behind you. Click and treat as the dog targets your hand with a nose touch. Repeat a few times.

3. Move your hand behind you and click and treat as your dog follows your hand.

4. When your dog is moving behind on a reduced hand signal begin to put in the cue word, such as 'hide'.

Marie teaches Cookie how to 'hide' in a high-distraction area

Related ideas...   **24**   **25**   **26**   **44**   **46**

Introduce time spent alone

It is useful for all dogs to learn to spend time on their own. It gives your dog the opportunity to calm, settle down and sleep if he is getting grumpy or over-excited. There may also be times in your dog's life when he cannot be with you, so it is only fair to teach him how to accept this calmly from an early stage.

Time spent alone should not be distressing for your dog

Avoiding loneliness

Start by leaving your dog for very short periods, while you are at home. Make sure that he has had the opportunity to go the toilet. Decide on a safe, secure area where he will be comfortable. Put the radio on low and give him a blanket or jumper, which bears your (recent) scent, as a comforter. Make sure the comforter is big enough for him to spread and lie down on if he wants to.

When you intend to leave your dog, be neutral and avoid over-interacting with him for a short time before you go. If you chat to him and cuddle him just before you leave your absence will distress him even more.

Your dog should be able to cope with being left alone for short periods

Leave something really tasty to occupy him. Keeping a special toy that is only given to your dog when you are out and that is picked up when you return home can help to make your absences less stressful.

Cookie is more than happy to be left alone with her Kong™

Gradually build up the time that your dog is on his own so that he can cope if for example you have to chat to a caller in a smart suit or leave the house on some other solo pursuit.

KEEP CALM

When you see your dog again, avoid the temptation to squeak an excited greeting and ruffle his coat wildly. Say hello quietly and be neutral until you have both calmed down; then calmly let him know how wonderful he is and how much you missed him.

IMPORTANT SKILLS

Related ideas... 1 55 58

58 Teach him to accept 'time out'

'Time out' is the opportunity to remove the reward of attention at times when your dog behaves inappropriately to get attention. Be honest and fair though. If your dog is being demanding because you have been too busy to give him quality time or if he has been left on his own for a while, it is only right to uphold your end of the relationship and spend some time playing with him or having a lovely relaxing TTouch session.

Cookie calls her own 'time out' during an exciting and energetic game

The most effective way to practise 'time out' is to get up and walk away, through a door and close it for two minutes. However, if there are other family members or pets in the room that your dog can harass, attach a light leash to your dog's collar when he seems likely to become over-active or demanding. If he starts mouthing or play biting, climbing on you or any other member of the household, calmly pick up the leash, walk him out of the room and shut the door behind him for two minutes. If he demands attention again as soon as he is allowed back in, repeat the short time out until the penny drops that rude, inappropriate behaviour loses everybody's attention.

If it is impractical to remove him or yourself, use the containment exercise (way 11) to quieten him.

TO MAKE IT WORK

Keep your body language neutral and avoid speaking or making eye contact. Even a glance may seem a good reward to your dog. To be effective, a time out needs to be short, that is no more than a couple of minutes. Shutting your dog away for an hour or so may make you feel better in the short term but your dog will not learn anything from the experience.

Related ideas…   **14**   **18**   **46**   **47**   **55**

Have a sensible bedtime routine

It goes without saying that your dog should be given the opportunity to go to the toilet before bedtime. Fast, exciting games are unlikely to put him in the mood for sleep, and again this is where some calming TTouches (pp.35–38) could help create a state of calm to prepare for a peaceful night.

Where is the bed?

It is entirely your decision where your dog sleeps. Ensure that his bed is in a practical place and that he is going to be warm and comfortable through the night. Many dogs settle very well in their indoor kennel or in the place where they are left alone at other times.

Dogs can happily share their owner's bedroom so long as they know how you expect them to behave and where you would like them to settle. If left to work out appropriate bedroom behaviour on his own, your dog might think he has some territorial rights and if he has nabbed your bed may growl when you toss and turn in bed or refuse you re-entry after an urgent nocturnal visit to the bathroom.

A really clever dog may also work out a very neat trick. He may scratch at the bedroom door to arouse you from your slumbers then as you pad, heavy-eyed to let him out of the room, he will nip neatly into the lovely warm space that you have so obligingly vacated. This is not your dog trying to 'pull rank' or 'be dominating'; it is you forgetting to teach him boundaries (see also way 60). To avoid this type of situation, always make sure he has his own bed or indoor kennel in the bedroom and that he knows that that is his place to settle.

Remember: a bedroom secret should be something that is between you and the man or woman of your dreams, not a vital piece of petiquette that you somehow forgot to teach your dog.

IMPORTANT SKILLS

It is useful to teach your dog to settle in his own bed, even if it is in your bedroom

Related ideas...   1   57   58

It is good manners to respect your dog's personal space and it is important that he learns to respect yours. We all love a cuddle but there are times we just want some peaceful distance without having to shut a dog out of the room.

IMPORTANT SKILLS

Containing Cookie

When Cookie first came to Tilley Farm on foster she was really, really demanding. She had learnt to grab and mouth hard to get attention. It was impossible to work if Cookie was in the office. Although she was coming along well with her training, if Sarah was sitting at the desk, Cookie would literally launch herself at her, barking and snapping to get attention. It is very hard to refrain from giving attention to a dog when they are hanging off your hands and causing serious bruising.

Sarah put some sticky tape across the floor and clicker-trained Cookie to stay one side of the tape until she was called over to have some attention. This was a fun game for Cookie and a very practical one for Sarah. The tape defined a very clear boundary for Cookie, and her bed and a chew toy were left on the far side so that she had plenty of good things on the other side of the tape. You can use a similar method to ensure that your dog understands your boundaries.

Sarah is extending Cookie's training to the outside world and no longer needs a length of sticky tape to set a boundary

Related ideas…  1 57 58

Silver Certificate

Silver certificate – key skills

The exercises and games in this section build on the basic skills your dog has already mastered. They are an important progression from the Bronze certificate exercises and are a bridge to the more advanced exercises in the Gold certificate section.

We have included more games as well as follow-on exercises, such as stand/sit and down stay, the target stick, working with another person and being led by a child, to give you plenty of choices in the way that you continue with your dog's education.

If your dog (or you!) are struggling at any point during this section go back to the easier training exercises in the Bronze section to consolidate your skills. If there has been a break in the training for any reason it is a good idea to revisit the earlier exercises to ensure that your dog has a clear understanding of what each cue means and is offering consistent behaviours before moving on through this section.

More games & groundwork

Beginning on p.113, these are some more fun exercises to keep your clever hound active and entertained.

You are well on the way to getting your Silver Certificate, but don't rush, there's still plenty of work to be done, and you want to be sure that you both enjoy the games and continue to learn together every step of the way.

---

100 Ways to Train the Perfect Dog

Silver Certificate

This is to certify that

Owner: _____ & Dog: _____

Have successfully completed training to become a perfect dog [and owner!] Well Done!

Sarah and Marie

61 Habituate him to being handled by another person

Once your dog or puppy is happy to be touched all over his body, you can continue his education by enlisting the help of a friend.

Getting your dog accustomed to being handled by other people is essential preparation for visiting the groomer or the vet. The TTouches (pp.35–38) are fantastic for this exercise as they provide something that is consistent and they have a relaxing effect on the dog.

Monty can be a little shy when it comes to being handled by a second person. He licks Sarah's hand, which can be a sign of concern

1. Let your dog approach the other person so that he can introduce himself appropriately to your friend.

2. If your dog is nervous, introduce the second person by playing a game that he knows with your friend standing quietly by and watching, or going for a walk together.

3. Try putting a second leash on your dog and have your friend take it while you walk around together. You can use the clicker and treats if necessary so your dog learns that other people are not a threat and that good things happen when another person is near by.

Watch his body language and take your time. Show your friend how to approach your dog and ask them to use the back of their hand to initiate contact. It is really important that your friend does not lean over and/or stare at the dog.

If your dog is happy, ask your friend to handle him gently all over his body. Sarah uses TTouches to help Monty become more confident

Related ideas…    **11**   **12**   **41**

Introduce grooming by a second person

It does not automatically follow that your dog will enjoy being groomed by a second person just because a friend or family member can now handle him all over (way 61). If he will not allow a second person to groom him, he will loathe going for a cut and blow dry. The grooming parlour will not be that thrilled to see him either.

Every time we change one thing, we potentially change everything, so some dogs that enjoy being groomed by their favourite person may still be concerned if someone else approaches them with a brush.

Begin by following the steps in way 61. If your dog is happy to be touched all over, your friend can go ahead and spruce up your pooch with his usual grooming brush. If he is a little reticent give your friend a sheepskin mitt or a Jelly Scrubber™ (see p.141) and show them how to do some TTouches with it.

Watch your dog's expression all the time. He may be still because he is happy but he may be still because he has gone into 'freeze' (p.32). If he is in 'freeze', ask your friend to stop, then take your dog and walk him quietly away.

Related ideas... 11   12   50

Teach 'sit stay'

63

Now that your dog is reliably offering sit, start delaying the click for a few seconds to extend the time that he remains in the sitting position – introducing him to the idea of 'stay'. He will quickly learn that the treat does not appear if he moves before hearing the click. Gradually extend the time that you are asking him to maintain the sit but vary the times so that they do not become predictable to him.

When you start the exercise, if he does move, wait for a moment to see if he can work things out for himself – hold fire and see if he offers the sit again. If he does sit, click and treat after a few seconds. If he is struggling to understand what you want, it may be necessary to encourage him to sit again by offering the signal that you have already taught him.

When your dog is able to maintain the sit for two minutes, start giving a verbal and visual cue. Quietly say 'sit stay' while simultaneously giving a flat hand signal at your chest height. There is no need for you to shout the verbal cue or put your flat hand in front of his face to reinforce your desire for him to stay in the sit position.

Extend the time that your dog remains in the sit position

Related ideas... 25

64 Progress to 'down stay'

Now that your dog is consistently offering the down on cue, delay the click for a few seconds to extend the time that he remains in position. He will quickly learn that no treat appears if he moves before he hears the click.

If your dog moves, as mentioned in 'sit stay', give him the opportunity to work it out for himself. If he corrects himself and offers the down again, click and treat after he has maintained the position for a few seconds. However, if he is struggling to understand, it may be necessary to encourage him to 'down' again by offering the down signal.

Gradually extend the time that you are asking him to maintain the down, until he can do it for up to about three minutes but vary the times so that they do not become predictable. Use the stay cue described in the 'sit stay' exercise (p.103).

Related ideas...   17

65 Introduce 'stand stay'

Once your dog is reliably offering the 'stand' you can teach him to stay in that position. You will be using the same steps as in the other 'stay' exercises. Gradually extend the length of time that you are asking him to maintain the stand, but vary the times so that they are not predictable to the dog. This will help him to stay engaged and not anticipate anything.

Give him the cue to stand and start delaying the click for a few seconds to extend the time that he remains in the standing position. He will quickly learn that no treat appears if he moves before he hears the click.

If he moves, give the dog the opportunity to work the exercise out for himself so wait for a moment to see if he offers the stand again. Click and treat after a few seconds. If he is still struggling to understand what you are asking, it may be necessary to encourage him to stand again by offering the stand signal.

Remember to use your stay cue.

Related ideas...   28   63   64

Consolidate 'stays' using distractions

The icing on the cake is to consolidate your stays by introducing some distractions while your dog is in a stay position.

Many owners find that a long-practised stay tumbles like the proverbial house of cards because their dog is used to doing a stay in one location only, and when everything is still and quiet, too. If asked to stay in a different location where there may be unusual noises, movement and tempting things, your previously impeccably behaved canine may appear to be disobedient when he breaks the stay. In truth, he is doing exactly what you taught him to do, which is to maintain the position in one familiar (unrealistic) environment.

1. Start with your dog on the leash at your side and ask him to 'stay'.

2. Drop a low-value toy or a treat a couple of paces away. If he tries to move forward, half-step in front of him and pick up the toy or treat before he reaches it.

3. Repeat the exercise until he is able to maintain the position for a couple of seconds without moving.

4. Now step forward and pick up the toy or treat and step back to him, give your 'Finish' cue and reward him.

5. Gradually build up the time he is able to stay.

Engage the help of friends or family to create some distractions. Start with small easy steps and gradually increase the level of distraction, making sure that you reward your dog well for resisting temptation.

Finally, make sure that you practise all stays, with and without distractions, in several different locations so that your dog can understand and consolidate the sit, down and stand stay.

Extend the exercise by using food. Ensure the leash is loose and that your dog is truly in a 'sit stay'

Ask your dog to sit and stay and throw a toy a short distance away

Marie rewards Maisie by picking up the toy and bringing it back to her

Related ideas...   **54**   **63**   **64**   **65**

Practise allowing him to be led away from you

A secure dog will happily trot off with a person who is with you, and not become alarmed. Clingy dogs that are permanently glued to their owner's side will often develop separation anxiety as they mature, so this is an important exercise to teach your dog as it will allow you to monitor his confidence levels.

SILVER CERTIFICATE – KEY SKILLS

Making a start

Stay neutral in both your voice and body language, so as not to give your dog cause for concern. The second person should also be calm and confident.

1. Walk forward with the second person, then hand over his leash and his treat bag/toy – let your dog see that you are doing this and allow the second person to lead him away looking in the direction in which they are moving and not back towards you.

Marie, Sarah and Naomi are walking in the park with Orsa, Cookie and Fluffy. Orsa is more than happy to walk close to Naomi's side, even though she belongs to Sarah, who is walking next to her and is engaged with a small potential usurper

2. The person can reward the dog for giving them his attention by playing a game with his toy or food from his own treat bag.

3. When your dog has moved away a short distance, the person should lead him back and allow him to check in with you. Remain neutral and continue to repeat the exercise to increase his confidence.

We are not suggesting for a second that you should encourage your dog to wander off with a perfect stranger; that would be foolhardy and dangerous. However, he should have the confidence to settle with a person known to you both, especially if they have clearly been entrusted with his favourite toy and/or treat bag.

Orsa happily goes off for a walk with Naomi

Related ideas...   **25**   **26**   **41**   **61**

Teach him to be led by a child

Children love to be involved in the process of taking the family dog for a walk, and even if they are very small there is a way to include them, without putting the child or dog at risk of accident or injury.

Harry is not used to such a big dog so starts by walking a little behind Orsa

1. You will need an extra leash that you can thread through the collar or, better still, attach it to a harness in addition to your normal walking kit. Attach one leash to the collar and one to the harness. If you only have a collar on your dog, loop a leash through the collar. Make sure that the two leashes are not clipped onto the same ring and do not use two separate collars.

2. Make sure you have the controlling leash on one side and allow the child to hold a neutral leash on the other side. Now you are in a perfect position to make sure that the child is not pulled over and your dog is not dragged around by an over-enthusiastic youngster.

When things go well, Harry becomes braver and more confident

Related ideas…   **23**   **25**   **26**   **43**   **61**

69 Discover successful fetch or retrieve

This is an extension of the shared game that you taught your dog in way 18. Now he knows the joy of sharing a game with you and does not feel threatened if he has anything in his mouth when he is around you, you are going to shape a more controlled retrieve using the clicker and this will form the basis of some of our future exercises.

Starting work

1. Sit on a chair or stool and drop one of your dog's toys on the floor just in front of you. When he looks at it, click and treat. Repeat this a couple of times.

2. When your dog looks at and then moves towards the toy, click and treat. Repeat a couple of times.

3. Wait until your dog moves forward and touches the toy. Click and treat and repeat a couple of times.

Cookie picks up the toy and returns it to Marie

4. Wait to see if he will then pick up the toy. Click and treat.

5. Withhold the click to encourage your dog to hold on to the toy for longer. If he drops the toy, stay neutral and wait until he has picked it up again and held it for a couple of seconds before you click and treat.

6. Continue to slowly shape the retrieve until your dog is consistently picking up the toy and then moving towards you with the toy in his mouth.

Cookie targets the toy

Cookie hears the click and looks for a treat

Shape the retrieve until your dog is picking up the toy and moving towards you

Increasing the skill level

The next stage is to put one hand under or on the toy while it is in your dog's mouth; click as the dog releases it directly into your hand and treat (make sure the clicker is in your other hand and well away from the dog's ears!).

Continue to shape this behaviour until your dog is able to take up the sit position on cue while still holding the toy. Be patient; some dogs find it easier to multi-task than others (and trust us, this has nothing to do with whether they are male or female!).

Now shape the behaviour until your dog retrieves when you are in a standing position too. Remember to keep your body language neutral. Avoid staring directly at him or leaning over towards him as he approaches you.

When your dog understands what is required, begin to add a retrieve cue such as 'fetch' or 'pick it up' ('Pick it up?' We hear you cry, 'Surely dogs can only work with single, one-syllable words?' 'Not true', we cry back.)

Now you can begin to throw the toy and he knows exactly how to bring it back for his reward of a game or a treat.

Oz (and Marie) are enjoying the benefits of a game on the beach. Teaching a fetch and retrieve enables you to keep your dog engaged with you when out and about, and gives him more physical and mental stimulation than he would get by simply walking by your side

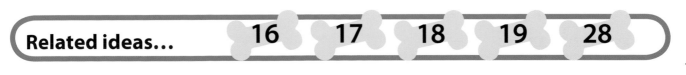

Related ideas... **16** **17** **18** **19** **28**

Move on to multiple retrieves

Now your dog is having fun returning to you with one article it is time to 'up the ante' and teach him how to retrieve multiple toys that are thrown at the same time. Try to play with toys of different textures and materials so that he learns to carry a variety of different articles.

The idea of retrieving several articles can be confusing for some dogs, so start with just two thrown a short distance away and gradually build up his confidence until he can retrieve up to half a dozen articles one after the other.

If he is reluctant to pick up any particular texture go back to way 18 – playing the shared game to encourage your dog to enjoy retrieving anything he is asked to bring back.

Multiple retrieves are more of a challenge

Give him a verbal cue, such as 'dead', to let him know that the article is now out of play and encourage him to retrieve another article

ENSURE YOU GET ALL THE TOYS BACK

Make every single article your dog brings back exciting and rewarding. Stop and play briefly with each one he returns, or at the very least tell him how wonderful he is before asking him to go back for another. If most retrieves are taken for granted by you and are not fun or rewarding to him, the game will become boring for most dogs.

Related ideas... **18** **19** **69**

Teach acceptance of tethering

Tethering is a great self-control exercise for your dog, and you never know when it might be useful or necessary to tether him for a few minutes, in an emergency for example. It can also help him to learn the comfort benefits of maintaining a loose leash.

Cookie is quite happy to sit tethered to the fence

1. Use a standard flat collar, or preferably a harness and make sure you use a quick-release knot in the beginning. Be ready with your clicker and treats.

2. Ask your dog to sit or stand. If he moves, stay quiet and as soon as the leash shows any slack at all; click and drop a treat – make sure it is within his reach!

3. Repeat this a couple of times, but keep the sessions short; aim for confidence and success. As your dog gains confidence, gradually increase the distance that you move away from him.

4. When this is accepted, pop out of sight. If the exercise has been built up slowly, your dog should remain calm with a slack leash so that a helper nearby can click and treat.

Important note
We definitely do not advocate tethering your dog outside a shop, however friendly and well-behaved he might be in this situation. He will be a sitting target and may be teased by passing children or even an unpleasant adult and sadly many unattended dogs are stolen these days.

Related ideas...   63   66

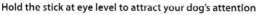

72 Use a target stick

Teaching your dog to follow a target stick is an extension of the hand target (way 24) and enables you to begin to work him at more of a distance. It is particularly useful for practising following and loose leash walking when you have a small dog, as it removes the need to bend over the dog, making the exercise less intimidating for the dog and much easier on your back.

You can buy ready made target sticks from various sources, or make your own. The one we are using is a telescopic magnet, which can be purchased very cheaply from a hardware store. It has a brightly coloured cat toy fitted neatly over the magnet at the end. This target stick can be used at varying lengths so is both versatile to handle and attractive for the dog to follow.

1. Hold the target stick vertically so that the ball is at eye level to your dog; as he looks at the ball, click and treat.

Marie clicks before Layla opens her mouth and tries to grab the toy

Hold the stick at eye level to attract your dog's attention

2. When your dog moves towards the target, click and treat. Make sure that you click before he opens his mouth and attempts to grab it.

3. Begin to move the target around slowly; click and treat as your dog follows it.

Progress at a rate that will maintain your dog's interest. Be creative and think of uses for the target stick, including tricks you might be able to teach, such as circling left or right perhaps.

Related ideas… 24 27

Work with the teeter-totter

The teeter-totter is a progression from the walk-over board (way 35) and is a low-level see-saw that is easily made out of wood if you are handy with a saw, hammer and nails.

Teaching your dog to walk over a moving surface improves balance, co-ordination and self-control. It is also helpful for dogs that are worried about travelling in a car, which in some cases can be linked to poor stability. You can incorporate this exercise into jumping over poles, the walk-over board and raised poles on the ground so that you create your own mini-agility course.

(Left and below) Sally is walking over the teeter-totter, which will help her to become more confident in a car

1. Start by placing two blocks or bricks under each end of the teeter-totter so that it does not move. Use a harness, flat collar and double-clipped leash on your dog.

2. Remove one block so that the board goes down when your dog first steps onto it.

Walk him to the middle of the board and ask him to stand or sit. Then ask him to walk off the end.

3. Remove the second block and repeat step 2, making sure that you teach your dog to go over the see-saw from both directions. You want him to walk calmly and slowly over the teeter-totter.

4. You can then ask him to go over the teeter-totter off leash.

Related ideas... **34** **35** **36**

Teach jumping off-leash

Once your dog is happily walking over low-level poles (way 34) you can teach him to jump over low fences off-leash. Most dogs enjoy jumping, and this exercise teaches them to focus on your hand position and to stay engaged with you. You can easily purchase small cones and poles from the internet or a sports' shop that sells soccer equipment for training. Make sure that you do not over-face your dog by asking him to jump obstacles that are too high or by asking him to perform if he is sore or uncomfortable through the shoulders, back or hindquarters.

MORE GAMES & GROUNDWORK

Here goes...

Set up your jumps in a large rectangle or octagon, making them no more than 15cm (6in) high to start. This will help him to understand that you want him to jump rather than ducking around the side of the fence.

1. Step over the poles and encourage your dog to follow. Click while he is jumping and treat him when he lands.

2. Once he is happy jumping in and out of the square or octagon, ask him to sit and stay on one side of the jump. Go to the other side of the jump and call him. As he jumps give him a cue such as 'up' or 'over'. Remember to click and treat him.

Cookie is having fun learning to negotiate low jumps with Marie

You can vary the exercise by standing in the middle and using your hand to direct him over the jumps.

If your dog steps over with his front paws and then gets 'stuck' use the zigzag TTouch (p.38) along his back and down his hindquarters.

Calgacus LOVES jumping!

Tracey calls Calgacus over the jump and rewards him with a treat

Related ideas...   24   34   73

Play with the Dog Tornado

Remove all thoughts of English Bull Terriers hurtling down the hallway to greet homecoming family members. This Nina Ottosson dog toy (p.21) is a step on from the Dog Spinny (way 32).

The principles of this game are the same as the easier exercise but now the dog has three layers to swivel with his nose and thus more yummy treats to find.

Archie negotiates three layers with his nose

Related ideas...   32   33

Learn the Dog Smart together

Or 'Smart Dog', which is now Archie's official middle name. Archie loves this Nina Ottosson toy (p.21) the most and, as he is very dexterous with his mouth, it gives him an appropriate outlet for this supreme skill, which is far more appealing than his old habit of thieving a jar of fresh pesto from the kitchen counter and delicately unscrewing the lid without leaving a single tooth mark on it.

To play with this toy, the dog needs to pull out each block to access the hidden treats. They should not be encouraged to push them over with their paw.

1. Load the toy while your dog is watching. Sit with him and show him that the treats are hidden beneath the wooden blocks. Let him work it out for himself but do not let him go charging around the living room or garden with the blocks. They are not his prize.

2. Encourage and praise your dog as he gets closer to the goal.

Vary the game and only place treats under a few blocks and see if he can work out which ones are covering up the treats.

Sarah shows Archie where the treats are hidden (above). He carefully removes the block ... and voila! has found the treat

Related ideas...   32   33   75

Enjoy weave poles together

Panic not. This exercise is not part of focused agility work that needs you to learn some specific body posture in order to train your dog. It is simply a fun way to help him extend his focus and learn another new skill while flexing his body and gaining freedom of movement through his ribs.

MORE GAMES & GROUNDWORK

1. Wait until sunset and take your weave poles to a gorgeous beach. (If you do not live near a beautiful beach, your garden will do just fine.)

2. Set them in a line and teach your dog to negotiate the poles while on a leash.

3. Then hold a treat in the hand that is nearest to the poles and ask your dog to follow your hand.

Give him regular treats while he is learning the exercise. Remember to work in both directions and make sure that you are not blocking his path by leaning over or standing in front of your dog.

Start by negotiating the poles together, with your dog on the leash

Ask your dog to follow your hand

Related ideas...   **22**   **23**   **24**   **34**

Silver Certificate

Wow!!! We are impressed! Well done. Copy your Silver Certificate (p.101), stick it on your fridge and do not let any visiting friends or family sit down or eat or drink anything until they have admired it for at least 10 minutes.

Gold Certificate

Gold Certificate – key skills

You've reached the final leg of your training journey. Even if it has taken you some time to get here you should be really proud of your achievements so far, and by now you will have a dog that is the envy of all your friends.

Gold and beyond

There are just a few more exercises to teach your dog and then some added extras to pick from (p.126). You have already achieved some remarkable results and your partnership should be well and truly established. You should be immensely proud of everything that you have achieved together and your dog should now be a sociable, content and happy hound, whether you are relaxing at home together, exploring the great outdoors or engaged in a variety of social events.

If your dog still has concerns about certain aspects of his life, please do not feel disheartened. By teaching him the Bronze and Silver exercises you have given him a good foundation on which other life experiences can still be built. Dogs have different personalities just like humans and their unique characters are there to be enjoyed. Remember that they continue to learn throughout their life and you may be amazed at how your dog continues to grow in confidence as he matures. We both own dogs that have needed lots of understanding and reassurance at times, largely because they were so incredibly fearful when they first came to live with us. If you think that you have not got anywhere with your dog and will never be able to teach him these more advanced exercises, pause for a moment and look back. When you remember your early days together, you will realize just how far you have come. Teach him the fun exercises such as jumping or tidying up for example and then go back to the Gold key skills at the beginning of this section or revisit the earlier exercises in the Bronze and Silver sections.

Remember that your dog does not care what other people think of him, he only has eyes for you.

---

100 Ways to Train 🦴 the Perfect Dog

Gold Certificate

This is to certify that

Owner: _____ & Dog: _____

Have successfully completed training to become a perfect dog [and owner!] Well Done!

Sarah and Marie

Gold Certificate – Key skills

Begin working on 'sit stay out-of-sight'

78

Once your dog can maintain a two-minute sit in sight (way 63), it is time to progress this exercise. Here you are going to teach him to sit and stay while you are out of sight.

1. Set up your dog to do a sit stay 8–10 paces away from something that you can duck behind or somewhere you can easily move out of sight. Remember to give him the sit stay cue.

2. Disappear from your dog's view for a few seconds then walk back and reward him.

3. If your dog is settled repeat this step.

Build up gradually so that he is able to cope with you being out of sight for at least one minute of the two-minute sit stay.

Move behind a tree or wall so that you are out of sight

Related ideas...　　16　63　66

79

Try 'down stay out-of-sight'

The steps to this exercise are the same as the sit stay out-of-sight' (way 78). If your dog is nervous but is the type of dog to internalize his concerns, he may stay as asked but prefer to stand or sit. If he does, go back to the easier down exercise (way 17) and use a bodywrap or T-shirt to help him feel more secure.

1. Set up your dog up to do a down stay 8–10 paces from a place where you can hide.

2. Disappear from your dog's view for a few seconds then walk back and reward him, then walk away again.

3. If your dog is settled, repeat this step.

Gradually extend the time that you are out of sight so that he is eventually able to cope with you being away for at least two minutes of a three-minute down stay.

Hide so that you are out of your dog's view

Related ideas...　　26　64　66

Go hunting for treats

Games that use your dog's scenting ability are not only rewarding for him, but mentally tiring, which is rewarding for you too. This is a step up from the simple food scattering exercise (way 31).

1. Tether your dog (way 71) or have a helper hold on to him. Show your dog his favourite treats and let him see you move a short distance away. As you move away, keep bending down and touching the ground, sometimes leaving a treat and sometimes not so that he gets the idea of putting his nose down and checking the whole area.

2. Release him to go and search for his treats. Repeat a couple of times.

Tracey has released Oz and he is really using his nose to find the food

3. Now start hiding the treats in less obvious places. Let him see you disappear with the treats and then return to release him to find them. Now that he has to work harder, leave a random jackpot to really keep him keen – several yummy treats in a pile.

Scatter the food so that your dog can see you

GOLD CERTIFICATE – KEY SKILLS

Oz follows his nose around the corner and finds the jackpot

Related ideas...   27   31

81 Move on to chase recall

If your dog has a high chase drive, this is a good way to channel and control his chase instincts. It will also help you with your co-ordination, timing and awareness. You will need two identical toys that you are able to throw at a reasonable and controlled distance. Balls on ropes are brilliant, but ensure that your dog adores his ball on a rope, because the retrieve and subsequent shared game with you will be his reward. If he is keener to retrieve for a food reward, have his favourite goodies in the treat bag.

Throw toy 1 towards your helper

1. It is invaluable to have a second person to help with the early stages of this exercise. Make sure you have taught a solid retrieve (way 69).

2. Make sure your dog knows there are two toys. Ask your helper to stand approximately 20 paces away in the direction that you intend to throw toy 1 but slightly off to one side.

3. With your dog in a sit, hold either his collar or a short tab attached to his collar to ensure that he stays with you until released. Throw the toy reasonably near to but obviously not right on top of your helper.

4. Release your dog but call him to get his attention when he is just starting his run towards the toy. The chances are he will ignore you because he is so focused on the thrown toy. At this point your assistant should step forward, pick

If your dog moves towards toy 1, ask your helper to step forward and pick it up

Oz does a hand-brake turn when called, and is ready to chase the second toy

up the toy and stand in a neutral position, without talking to or making eye contact with your dog. Continue to call him and when you have his attention, throw toy 2 away from you, in the opposite direction from toy 1.

5. Allow him to chase it and bring it back to you. Have a wonderful shared game with that toy and tell him how marvellous he is or give him his favourite treat, depending on what floats his boat.

WHEN YOU DON'T HAVE AN ASSISTANT

If you do not have an assistant to help you with this exercise it can be carefully trained using a long line attached to a harness. Please make sure that you can judge the length of the line against the distance that you throw or you will be in danger of somersaulting after a dog who reaches the end of the line with his toy still way out of reach and he might be injured by a sudden tug on his collar.

6. Repeat a few times and your dog will begin to get the hang of the game. He should learn that he will have more fun chasing the second toy because he gets to run further and also because the chase will end with an additional reward of a game with his favourite person or a tasty treat.

7. Build the game slowly, increasing the distance toy 1 is thrown and the distance your dog is from you on his run towards it before you call him and throw the really rewarding article (toy 2) in the opposite direction.

The ultimate test is when you begin the game with your dog loose and he starts his run before toy 1 has landed, but work slowly towards this goal. Try to make sure that he does not win toy 1; his focus should be on the second toy that you throw because this is how he gains your full attention and receives the big reward.

Related ideas…   **18   19   69   70**

Progress to hunting for toys (play search)

You have already taught your dog to retrieve multiple articles or toys that have been placed in sight (way 70). You have also taught him to search for hidden treats (way 80). Now we are going to extend those two skills and encourage him to search for toys or other articles.

1. Remind your dog of the fun of the multi-retrieve game (way 70).

2. Now, while holding him, throw two articles into longer grass or onto an uneven surface. He will watch the first land but will mark the second.

3. Release him and ask him to 'find and fetch' (or 'find' and your retrieve cue). He will go straight to the second article because he has marked it. Encourage him to bring it back to you and have a really good, shared game or give him a high-value treat to reward him.

Oz follows the scent and finds his second toy

Marie has released Oz to find the hidden toys – he uses his nose to search the area and finds the toy HURRAH!!!!

4. Now say 'dead' and put the article in your pocket out of sight. Encourage your dog to go out and search for the other article.

As he becomes more confident, increase the number of articles you throw. When he really understands the game, tether your dog or have a helper hold on to him. Let him watch you place the articles, rather than throw them. He will learn to follow your scent trail as an additional help. If you are both having fun, increase the number of toys and make them more difficult to find. Avoid making it too challenging. Remember this is meant to be fun.

Related ideas... **69** **71** **81**

Play find the child

Children enjoy being invited to join in with training games and they LOVE this one. To start with have a second adult helper standing near the child to give direction and help with their confidence.

Hold your dog on a leash and allow him to watch the child disappear with his toy. When the child has hidden, encourage your dog to go and search for his toy, which is, of course, with the child. As your dog appears in sight, the second adult can prompt the child to throw the toy on the ground just to their side. If both dog and child are confident, you can then do this exercise off-leash.

Important note
Your dog must enjoy the company of children and not be frightened by them to participate in this game. If you have any doubt about how he will react when he comes upon a hidden child holding his toy, give it a miss!

GOLD CERTIFICATE – KEY SKILLS

Maisy hides and gets ready to throw Oz's toy as he finds her (above). When Oz is working off-leash, Maisy throws the toy to the side as he comes around the corner to find her (right)

Related ideas...   69   70   71   80   81

Teach creeping or crawling

This is not just a game to make your dog look cute. It can also be a very practical skill to teach. If your dog has bolted under your parked car or found himself stuck in a thicket, for example, he may be unwilling to come out if his back comes into contact with the car or bush when he tries to stand.

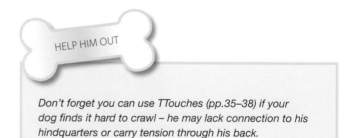

When your dog is in the down position, encourage him to crawl forward by drawing your hand forward a little

1. Ask your dog for the down position and place your hand flat on the floor with a treat underneath it. When he investigates your hand with his nose, click and treat.

2. Draw your hand forward a little and as he stretches his nose towards your hand he should start to crawl forward, click and treat. Repeat a few times.

3. Encourage him to target your hand, flat on the floor without a treat underneath. Click and treat.

Gradually increase the distance that he crawls forward when he is following your hand. Then begin to attach a verbal cue such as 'creep' or 'crawl'.

HELP HIM OUT

Don't forget you can use TTouches (pp.35–38) if your dog finds it hard to crawl – he may lack connection to his hindquarters or carry tension through his back.

Related ideas...   **17**   **24**

Introduce press the button

This is an easy and showy trick that can be used to finish a routine with a flourish or as a single skill. Both young and older dogs can pick up this game with astonishing ease. Once the dog has learnt to target with the button on the floor, you can hold the button against a wall. You can even fix a buzzer to the wall so that your dog learns to buzz when he would like to go out into the garden. You can purchase purpose-made buttons or buzzers, or use anything that can be pushed down with a paw.

1. Place the button on the floor. When your dog looks towards it, click and treat. If he approaches the button, regardless of how close he gets, click and treat

2. As soon as he is consistent in approaching the button to receive his treat, withhold the click and treat until he actually touches the button with his nose or paw. Build this up over several short sessions until your dog is consistently making contact with the button.

Fluffy soon learns that interaction with the button is the key to receiving the treat

If your dog approaches the button, click and treat

3. Now withhold the click unless the button makes a sound. Your dog will soon be banging the button, confident that the click will follow (a light bulb moment!).

4. When your dog is confidently offering what you want, begin to add a verbal cue, which can be any word of your choice. Finally, when the dog is consistent with the verbal cue, you can phase out the clicker and treat.

Wait until your dog touches the button before giving the treat

Related ideas…   **27**   **33**   **75**

86

Teach walk back or move away

This is a useful exercise to teach your dog how to move out of the way, and a great start to teaching tricks and doggy dancing.

1. Stand facing your dog, with your feet wide enough apart for him to fit through. Bend down and place a treat centrally on the floor just behind your feet – your dog will go to take the treat and then step back to look up at you in case there may be more food coming. As your dog steps back, click and treat. Repeat this several times.

Janet places a treat on the floor between and just behind her legs

Halo moves forward to pick up the treat

2. Begin to withhold the click as your dog steps back and wait to see what happens. Most dogs will take another step backwards. Click and treat.

As Halo steps back to see if there is another treat on its way, Janet clicks to mark the walk back

Halo is cottoning on and takes a few steps back

3. Build on this with more steps backwards and when the dog is confident begin to add a cue such as 'walk back' or 'move away'.

Related ideas...   56   92   93

Gold and beyond – More exercises to impress your family and friends

We are not going to be so mean as to make you teach your dog all the following exercises before you earn your Gold Certificate.

Once you have taught him the exercises in the Gold section, pick any two from the ways that follow. Then cook some liver cake or other fragrant goody for your pooch, buy a peg for your nose while you make the cake, get some treats for you and your friends and throw an enormous party with a huge photocopy of your Gold Certificate taking centre-place on your wall. (And email us a picture!)

Now is your chance to really start showing off. We have included some more fun exercises and some cool tricks to teach your dog and impress all who know you, plus give you the edge if you compete in a local fun dog show.

Inka and Maria enjoy a shared activity (left), while Cookie has learnt to work her own way through a line of poles (above)

Gold Certificate

Fanfare of trumpets (obviously muted if your dog is worried by noise). HURRAAHHH!!!! How smart is your pooch and how patient and clever are you? Nearly there now – keep going for a little longer and the certificate on p.117 is yours.

87 Play with an activity centre

Most dogs love to work through and under and over obstacles, through a tunnel, along a line of poles and so on. You can set up an exciting activity centre in your home or even build a permanent structure in your garden.

Set up an activity centre in your home

We have used a children's activity centre, which is inexpensive, fun and great for teaching spatial awareness. It can be used indoors or outdoors and can be broken down into different sections to help a more anxious dog to get used to the unusual shapes. Make sure that it is stable and won't move about too much to begin with. When the tunnel and tepees are put together, the dog can learn to negotiate from tent to tent via the tunnel.

Marie is teaching Fluffy to move in and out of a tepee

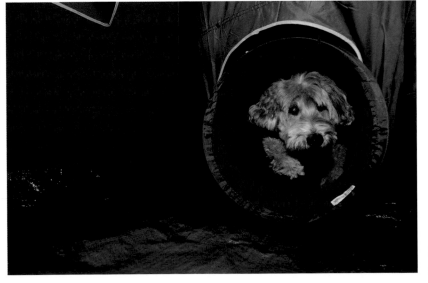

Fluffy has learnt to go through a tunnel

Related ideas... 81 82 84

Introduce carrying an article

Some dogs are naturally motivated to carry things in their mouth. This exercise gives them an outlet for this desire and can also be of benefit to you!

1. Place a small milk crate with empty plastic bottles on the floor and encourage your dog to target the handle as described in ways 72 and 85.

2. When he is confidently targeting the handle, withhold the click until he puts his mouth on the handle. Click and treat. Repeat a few times.

3. Wait until he picks up the crate by the handle, then click and treat. Repeat a few times.

Fluffy targets the crate handle   **Excellent!**

4. When he picks it up again, encourage him to move towards you. Don't panic if he drops the crate at any point or tries to grab the milk bottles. Stay neutral but click as soon as he picks up the crate again, to reinforce he is doing the right thing.

5. Continue to shape the behaviour until your dog can pick up the crate and bring it to you before you click. When he is confident with the whole skill, begin to add the cues you used for retrieve (way 69) and release (way 14).

If you want to increase the weight of the crate begin to put water into the bottles but make sure that the crate is balanced and not made lop-sided by the water.

CARRY A BASKET

This is the same principle as the milk crate so you need to go through the same steps. You can also combine this exercise with the tidy up game (way 94) so that your dog not only learns to put all his toys in one basket, but then puts the basket away as well.

Related ideas...   **14**   **69**   **72**   **85**   **94**

89 Teach removing a handkerchief from a pocket

OK – so we are showing off a little now but this exercise could help you win a class at a fun dog show and will certainly be of benefit if you ever succumb to a cold.

1. Encourage your dog to pick up a handkerchief from the floor and return it to your hand as described in the fun retrieve exercise (way 69).

2. Put the hankie in your pocket with most of it protruding and encourage your dog to target it using the clicker.

3. Now ask him to remove it from your pocket to give it to you.

4. Gradually reduce how much hankie is showing and repeat until your dog is really confidently pulling it out and handing it to you.

5. Begin to cue the behaviour by pretending to sneeze.

Repeat until he is confident and then dispense with the clicker. Hey presto! You have a dog who will take a hankie from your pocket and give it to you when you sneeze.

Monty quickly learns to target Jo's hankie (left)...and hand it back to her (above)

Related ideas...   **27**   **69**   **72**

90 Play magic dishes

This is another good fun game that encourages your dog to use his initiative and his nose. It can also make meal times more interesting, if you can't scatter food outside.

1. Place some upturned plastic dishes or discs on the floor. Tether your dog in sight or get somebody to hold him on the leash and let him watch you place treats under the dishes. At first put a treat under at least half of them.

2. Let your dog sniff at the dishes. When he stops and indicates that he has the scent of a treat, lift the dish and let him take the treat.

3. Make it more difficult by putting treats under fewer dishes.

Fluffy has found a treat

Related ideas...   **80**   **85**

Practise playing with a skateboard

This is a fun game and a rather impressive one as well. It gives Inka and Maria something that they can enjoy together and certainly attracts a lot of attention. If you do practise this by the canal it is worth taking a water-loving dog with you who can retrieve all the people that wander off the towpath while staring agog at your supreme skills.

1. Steady the skateboard so that it does not move unexpectedly and startle your dog. Go through the stages as described in way 85 to encourage him to target the skateboard.

2. Progress to putting a paw on the skateboard, click and treat. Repeat a few times.

3. Continue to shape this behaviour until your dog puts two paws on the skateboard. Click and treat.

4. Now withhold the click and treat until he keeps his front feet on for a few seconds. Repeat and build his confidence and increase the time he is on the board.

5. When his two feet are on the board, gently move the board forward slightly, click and treat. Repeat a few times to build up his confidence and increase his time on the moving board. He needs to get used to 'walking' with either one or two of his hind legs, depending on what comes naturally to him.

6. Now move away from the skateboard and shape the actions of your dog putting his feet on the board and moving towards you.

Inka can push herself along with either her hind feet or her left front and back leg

A skateboarding dog!

BE FAIR AND WISE

• It's a good idea to start on a carpet or other non-slippery surface, so that the skateboard does not suddenly fly forward and startle your dog.

• Take time and be prepared to have plenty of patience. If you rush this game and the dog becomes worried by the skateboard it is not going to be any fun for him or you.

Related ideas...   **35**   **36**   **45**   **73**   **85**

Train circling left and right

This is another easy exercise to teach your dog and will help him to be more flexible through the body.

Tracey uses a clicker and treats to teach Calgacus to circle left

1. Using your right hand, hold a treat just in front of your dog's nose and slowly lure him around to the right. As he starts to move his feet, click and treat. Repeat a few times.

2. Take this a step further by luring his nose around past his tail so that his front and hind limbs start to step round in a circle. Click here but reward as he finishes the circle.

3. Repeat again, clicking just after the halfway point and rewarding at the end of the circle. Practise until the movement becomes smooth and you no longer need to lure with a treat and he is happily targeting your hand all the way around.

4. Introduce a verbal cue such as 'right twist' or 'right spin'. Use different cues for each direction.

Follow the same steps to teach him to circle left using your left hand.

She repeats the exercise teaching Calgacus to turn to the right

Related ideas... **24**

Do leg weaves together

This is a fun exercise that is an extension of hand targeting (way 24). It increases flexibility in your dog (and you) and even large dogs can learn this trick. Tracey McLennan, a friend and fellow TTouch Practitioner has even taught her stunning Mastiff Calgacus (see p.132) to leg weave and the improvement in his body posture has been immense.

Maria moves the lure hand to the other side of her leg to draw Inka through

3. As your dog gains confidence, make the hand signals less exaggerated so the visual cue becomes the leg movement and toe point. Finally, add a verbal cue, such as 'through' or 'weave'.

Mirror the same steps to teach him to go under your left leg. When he has gained confidence in both directions you can begin to slowly walk forward, encouraging him to weave as you move. The visual cues will become your knee bend and toe point.

1. With your dog on your left, step forward on your right leg, pointing your toe down. Tap the inside of your right leg with the palm of your right hand and as your dog moves forward to target, click and treat. Repeat a couple of times.

2. As the dog moves forward, move your right hand to the other side of your right leg, drawing him between your legs. Click as he moves through and treat when he is right through. Repeat a few times.

The toe point becomes the visual cue to support the verbal cue

Related ideas...  **24** **92**

Teach tidying up

This is a wonderful game that can be extremely practical too. Teaching your dog to place toys in a box or trolley is easier than you might think. Especially as you already have a dog that is becoming increasingly creative, and one that can retrieve and drop an article on cue.

1. Sit or kneel with a low-sided box or trolley between you and your dog. Throw a toy onto the floor on the dog's side of the box.

2. As he leans over the box to give it to you, click and drop the treat into the box. The toy should drop into the box as the dog looks for his treat.

3. Repeat a few times until he gets the hang of it.

4. Throw a couple of toys to the other side of the box. When he has put the first toy in and found his treat, encourage him to do the same with the second.

Increasing his skills

When he is confident about the game, you can start to be more random about the treats and reward only the best attempts. Stand up and gradually move a few paces away from the box so that he really does learn the required behaviour. When he knows what he is doing, attach a verbal cue such as 'tidy up' or 'put them away'.

Encourage your dog to retrieve a toy, thrown onto the ground on his side of the trolley

Fluffy enjoys a well-earned treat. Yum Yum!

Encourage your dog to retrieve another toy

Related ideas...

70

Introduce send-away and moving between two targets

If you have worked through the exercises diligently, you have already trained your dog to move to a target (way 27). This is a progression of that skill.

The send-away

1. Put a target mat, cone or pole on the ground and remind your dog how to target it by going through the steps described in way 27.

2. When he is confident enough to move decisively away from you in a straight line to the target, add a verbal cue such as 'go to' or 'away'. It may take a few short sessions to get to this stage.

Adding the second target

When your dog is happily going out to one target on cue, it is time to add a second target.

1. Place two identical targets 10 paces apart. Move six paces away from the targets. Stand facing them.

2. With your dog by your side, swivel your body to face the first target and send him directly to it. He should be confident with this exercise so you should not need to click and treat, but if you need to remind him click and either

Maria lines her body up with the first target and sends Inka to it

throw a treat or repeat the send away, this time already having placed a treat on the target so that you click as he reaches the target and eats the treat.

3. Now when you send your dog to the target, he should look he should look expectantly at you on arrival at the target. Use your body position and arm to re-direct him to the second target. When he begins to move towards this target, click and throw a treat.

4. Gradually withhold the click and treat for longer periods, encouraging him to get nearer and nearer to the second target.

5. When the penny drops and your dog understands that he is to move to the second target, click and treat. Repeat until he is really familiar with the exercise and then put in a verbal cue, for example 'go right'.

Keep practising until your dog is confident about going in one direction with your visual and verbal cue. Then train him to go the other way following the same process.

Maria redirects Inka to the second target

Related ideas...   **24**   **27**   **72**

If your dog is comfortable jumping over low-level poles, you can teach him to jump over larger fences in a line or on their own. Revise ways 34 and 74 if you feel you could both do with a refresher.

GOLD AND BEYOND

Inka flies over the jumps

1. Start off with a very low single jump. Ask your dog to sit and stay on one side of it.

2. Step over the jump, take a couple of paces, then turn to face your dog and call him towards you. Click as he goes over the jump and reward him when he gets to you. Repeat several times.

3. Use the cue that you taught him with the low-level poles.

4. Add more jumps in a line and try to extend his skill by doing a two or three jump recall.

5. Slightly raise the jumps, but keep it fun. If your dog runs around the side of the jumps, go back to using one jump or lower the jumps again.

Once your dog has got the hang of this, try placing a favourite toy or treat on the other side of the jump, return to your dog, release him from his stay and run alongside him as he goes over the jump to the toy or treat.

More jumps

Get a friend to help you and progress to doing this using two or three jumps. Set up a line of three small jumps, and ask your friend to go to the end of the line of jumps with your dog's favourite toy.

Set up your dog in a sit stay, down stay or stand stay at the first jump and then give a release command such as 'ok' or 'go'. Your friend should enthusiastically recall your dog, using the toy as encouragement. He or she should click and treat your dog for completing the jumps. Your friend can then set up your dog at their end and send him back to you. This is a fun way to practise send-away and recall.

Related ideas... 20 34 63 74 95

Ask him to give left and right paw

This is another pretty easy exercise to teach. Some dogs are naturally motivated to use their paws to express themselves and this gives them a useful outlet, instead of allowing them to mindlessly paw at you for attention. Mind you, as you have so diligently taught him the personal boundary exercise (way 60), he won't be doing this anymore will he?

Marie gives Sally a treat when she lifts her paw

1. Put a yummy treat on your hand with the palm facing upwards. Curl your fingers over the treat and hold it in front of your dog. He will probably investigate first with his nose and then try to open your hand with a paw. As soon as your dog lifts his paw to your upturned fist, click and give him the treat in your hand. Repeat several times.

2. Start being selective – only click and treat when he touches your left hand with his right paw. Repeat until he is consistently offering the right paw.

3. Try without a treat: as your dog lifts his paw to your fist, open your hand and hold his paw gently for a second or two, then click and treat.

4. Repeat the process with the opposite hand until he is consistently offering his right paw to your left hand and his left paw to your right hand.

5. Begin to put in distinguishing verbal cues such as 'paw and shake' or 'touch and tap' so that he learns to offer the correct paw to the correct cue.

Sally is quickly learning to give a paw

Related ideas... 6 15 24

98

Progress to 'high five' and wave

When your dog has learned to give his paws on cue, teaching him to 'high five' and wave is relatively easy.

Introduce the high five

1. Stand in front of your dog and cue him to touch the palm of your left hand with his right paw. Click and treat.

2. Change your hand position to the 'high five'. Click and treat any attempt he makes to lift his right paw to your left hand. Repeat until he understands the new high five shake with his right paw.

3. Repeat the process with the opposite hand until he is consistently offering right paw to left hand and left paw to right hand in the high five position.

4. Add the verbal cues such as 'high paw', 'high shake' or 'high touch'.

It's time to wave

Wave is an easy progression from high five. Kneel with your dog and give the visual cue for high five; as he lifts his paw, raise your hand a little so that he just misses connecting. Click and treat. Repeat several times.

As you continue to practise, move yourself to the standing position. Your dog is likely to hesitate with the paw in the air as he tries to touch your high five visual cue. Click and treat this because it prolongs the time his paw is in the air. Repeat several times. Finally, add a verbal cue, such as 'wave', and begin to move your hand so the visual cue looks like a wave.

Smart dogs love to learn, and Inka has a huge repertoire of impressive skills

KNEELING DOWN

If your dog is struggling to learn this exercise try kneeling on the floor instead of standing.

Marie is seeing if Sally can offer a high ten

Related ideas...

97

Have him roll over

This is a fun exercise that's easy to add at this stage as it builds on skills your dog should already have.

1. With your dog in a down position, encourage him to target your hand back over his shoulders. This will help him to begin to roll. Click and treat. Repeat a few times until he gains confidence. If he is reluctant or unsure, have a treat in the target hand to give further encouragement the first few times.

2. Repeat but withhold the click and move your hand further over his body so he is encouraged to roll right over. Click and drop the treat on the side he is rolling towards.

3. Repeat until he rolls confidently following the visual cue then begin to attach a verbal cue and reward on completion.

Oz follows the hand target towards his shoulder (top) and begins to roll over (below)

Related ideas...   17   24

---

100 Play jumping through hoops

Our final game. It is great fun teaching your dog to walk or jump through a hoop. You can use different sizes of hoop to help him to develop special awareness. If you have bonded with your dog teaching him all the fun games and exercises in this book, he is probably very keen to show you that he will happily jump through hoops for you.

1. Hold the hoop with the base resting near the floor and the top slightly angled towards your dog. Have a treat in your other hand and encourage him to move through the hoop to get it. Repeat a few times.

2. Raise the hoop slightly but keep it angled towards your dog so it is easier for him to jump through.

3. Gradually teach your dog to jump or walk through smaller hoops.

Fluffy jumps through the big hoop

A final word

As hard as we try to give our dogs the best life possible, circumstances may change at some point. You may have a child, baby or another person enter your life or you may be unable to give your dog everything that you hoped you could because of changes in your own health or the demands of a new and exciting job. Your dog may be the one to suffer ill-health and may develop conditions such as arthritis or sustain an injury. It pays to be aware that such problems may arise and to be prepared for them if they do.

When things change

If you or your dog are unable to enjoy long walks or rigorous exercise for whatever reason, the simple TTouch low level groundwork and body TTouches, the Nina Ottosson toys and the clicker training will help him to maintain a healthy mental and emotional state. The TTouches will also help him to recover from or adapt more quickly to any physical changes he may experience.

If your dog is well socialized and has bonded with you and other family members and friends through the exercises in this book, he will probably be able to take new situations in his stride and with careful planning, the arrival of a baby or other alterations to his home environment will not be a monumental catastrophe for him. In the case of a baby, for example, you can purchase CDs to help him become accustomed to the noise of a baby and you can teach him to walk alongside a buggy before the baby arrives.

Diet

We are what we eat, and the same is true for our dogs. Dog food is a very controversial subject and it is important to do your own research and work out a suitable diet for your dog that is practical for you and beneficial for him. Some people do not accept that there is a link between a dog's diet and his behaviour; we wholeheartedly disagree. Dogs that are fed on more natural foodstuffs that are additive and preservative free (whether prepared lovingly at home or purchased) are calmer, more focused, and easier to live with and train.

Do not be conned by wording on the packets that may infer that the ingredients are wholesome and try not to become bogged down with information-overload when you are researching this subject. Some dogs do well on an all-raw diet, some do not. If you want to feed a complete dry food, go for something that is as natural as possible. Food colouring, high salt content, preservatives, additives and junk have no place in any diet. Some will need more carbohydrate or protein than others and some cannot tolerate certain ingredients. If your dog is totally 'hyper' he may do well to have a protein meal followed by a carbohydrate meal an hour or so later. This will increase his serotonin levels, which will help him to relax.

Enjoy the journey

We have so enjoyed compiling this book and we hope that it gives you plenty of ideas in the way that you interact with your dog. There is one final point to consider when working with your faithful friend. While it is good to aim for specific goals, having one eye set solely on the destination only leaves one eye for the journey. And it is the journey that creates a deep and everlasting bond.

Cookie has matured into the perfect companion and has now been adopted by Sarah

Further information

About TTouch

TTouch was developed over 30 years ago by animal expert Linda Tellington Jones, There are over a thousand Tellington TTouch practitioners working in 27 different countries. It is used by a variety of dog handlers and trainers, including those working with service, competition and family dogs, veterinarians, dog walkers, groomers, shelter helpers, behaviour counsellors and veterinary nurses.

Further reading and educational CDs

Unlock Your Dog's Potential
   Sarah Fisher, ISBN 978-0-7153-2638-1
Getting in TTouch with Your Dog
   Linda Tellington Jones, ISBN 1-872119-41-7
Clicker Training for Dogs
   Karen Pryor, ISBN 1-86054-282-4
Haynes Dog Training Manual
   Carolyn Menteith, ISBN 1-844253-51-1
The Canine Commandments
   Kendal Shepherd, ISBN 978-1-874092-55-1
On Talking Terms with Dogs: Calming Signals
   Turid Rugaas, ISBN 978-1929242368
Blue Dog Interactive CD is particularly good for teaching children about dogs. It is available from www.thebluedog.org, which also sells sound therapy CDs, see suppliers.

Suppliers

Jelly Scrubbers – www.tail-tamer.com also available in the UK
Kong toys – www.kongcompany.com for information on choosing and using these toys
Nina Ottosson Interactive toys – for a list of suppliers see www.nina-ottosson.com also available from www.companyofanimals.co.uk
Body wraps – available from www.ttouchteam.co.uk and www.ttouch.com
T-Shirts – the best fitting that we have found come from www.equafleece.co.uk
Fun training T-Shirts – www.K9byigloo.co.uk
Sound Therapy CDs – www.soundtherapy4pets.com
Training leashes – www.ttouchteam.co.uk and www.companyofanimals.co.uk
Training equipment – www.companyofanimals.co.uk

Useful Addresses

Robyn Hood
TTouch Canada
5435 Rochdell Road
Vernon BC1VB 3E8
www.tteam-ttouch.ca

Linda Tellington Jones
TTouch USA
PO Box 3793
Santa Fe
New Mexico 87501
USA
www.ttouch.com

Eugenie Chopin
TTouch South Africa
www.ttouchsa.co.za

Sarah Fisher
TTouch UK
Tilley Farm,
Bath BA2 0AB
01761 471182
www.ttouchteam.co.uk
email: sarahfisher@ttouchteam.co.uk

Marie Miller
61 Grange Road
Longford
Coventry
West Midlands CV6 6DB
02476 366090
www.pawsnlearn.com
email: ttouch@pawsnlearn.com

Maria Johnston
13 Spa Lane
Hinckley
Leicester LE10 1JA
01455 457350

Association of Pet Dog Trainers
www.apdt.co.uk

Acknowledgments

With thanks to Shelley Hawkins and Harley and Maisie Williams, Tina Constance and Sally, Jo Ors, Monty and Zack, Tracey McLennan, Calgacus and Cuillin, Maria Johnston and Inka, Janet Atkins and Halo, Naomi and Bob Atkins, Harry and Rachael Denness and Monty, Battersea Dogs and Cats Home, North Road Veterinary Centre, Jon Langley, Clare Edwards and Chilli, Jane Trollope and of course the FABULOUS and ever patient Jo Weeks.

About the authors

Sarah Fisher is the UK's only TTouch Instructor and has worked with a variety of dogs over the past 14 years. She has featured in many television programmes, including, *The One Show* (BBC1), *Animal Rescue Live* (BBC1) and *Talking to Animals* (ITV1 and Nat Geo). Sarah has written articles for *Your Dog* and *Dogs Today* and is the author of *Unlock Your Dog's Potential* (D&C, 2007). She teaches workshops for the UK's top shelters and lectures internationally and in the UK, Sarah also fosters over-the-top puppies for Battersea Dogs and Cats Home. She lives with her partner Anthony Head and their two daughters Emily and Daisy in a multi-dog household with Archie, Orsa, Ginny, Bud and Cookie.

Marie Miller has 30 years of practical experience of training dogs, including helping dogs assist their disabled owners, and is a qualified Tellington TTouch Practitioner 3 for Companion Animals and one of the founder members of the United Kingdom Association of Pet Dog Trainers (APDT 130). She has been the resident Pet Behaviourist and Trainer at Hollycroft Vet Centre, Hinckley, Leicestershire for the past 18 years and has had articles published in *Dogs Monthly*, *Dog Training Weekly* and *Service Dog*.

Marie shares her home with some of the stars of this book The Fluffy Stuffy, Our Oz and Maisy (German Shepherds), Tad (Dalmation x Labrador) and until recently Gem, who died on 30th January just short of her 14th birthday, and to whom this book is dedicated.

Marie says of Gem, 'She truly was the perfect dog and my son's best friend. At 13 years old he convinced us that he could be responsible for his own dog. He is an only child and we felt that it would be good for him to have a friend and confidant to help him through his teenage years.

'My dear friend Debbie Summers bred Gem and gave her to Sean as a gift, along with a stern lecture that if he ever let his special friend down in any way she would come and take the pup away again. Sean never let Gem or Debbie down – in fact I became a bit jealous that he was still getting up early to make scrambled eggs for her breakfast when she was eight months old! He came home from school every lunch time to see her, took her to training classes and trained her to the standard that she could demonstrate at Crufts in the DOGAID team with him when she was only 14 months old and he was only 14 years old. Gem was not at all surprised that her normally able-bodied friend was working her from a wheelchair. Gem did all Sean ever asked of her training wise but most of all she was his companion and best friend. She was the light of his life and he is still feeling lost without her company.'

Cookie Dough Dynamo is the real star of the book. She belonged to Battersea and has now been adopted by Sarah. Marie and Sarah have worked with Cookie to help her overcome her rather exuberant and inappropriate behaviour and she has matured into a delightful, charming and well-socialized companion while enjoying every aspect of her training.

Sean and Gem

Cookie Dough Dynamo

INDEX